www.ingramcontent.com/pod-product-compliance
Lightning Source LLC
Chambersburg PA
CBHW042353070526
44585CB00028B/2913

I Love Arabic series
Kindergarten (Part one)

Published By:
Arabic Joyride Press

We are proud to announce that this workbook is being distributed to the **Australian Arabic Academy**, supporting their mission to promote Arabic language and culture. Our sincere thanks to the Academy for their partnership and dedication to Arabic education.

Written by:
Widad Salman & Kawthar Joudeh

Illustrated by:
Kawthar Joudeh

Copyright © 2024 Arabic Joyride Press
All rights reserved.
ISBN: 978-1-7636023-2-8

*The copying of this book, in whole or in part, without the written consent of the authors, is not permitted.

سلسلة أنا أحب العربية – المرحلة التمهيدية (الجزء الأول)
نشر بواسطة

Arabic Joyride Press

نحن فخورون بالإعلان عن أن هذا الكتاب يتم توزيعه من خلال الأكاديمية الأسترالية للغة العربية، دعماً لمهمتهم في تعزيز اللغة والثقافة العربية. نقدم شكرنا الجزيل للأكاديمية على شراكتهم واهتمامهم بتعليم اللغة العربية

تأليف :
وداد سلمان وكوثر جودة

تصميم :
كوثر جودة

جميع الحقوق محفوظة : Arabic Joyride Press
ISBN: 978-1-7636023-2-8

نسخ هذا الكتاب كلياً أو جزئياً دون موافقة خطية من المؤلفين غير مسموح به

Parents' and Teachers' Guide

Kindergarten - Part one

Unlock the joy of learning Arabic with your child or student through this engaging and colourful book! Filled with fun exercises and vibrant illustrations, this book makes learning Arabic an exciting adventure.

What's Inside:

This workbook is part of the 'I Love Arabic - Kindergarten' series, published by Arabic Joyride Press. It is the first part and covers 1the first 7 Arabic letters. Each letter is introduced as an individual lesson with a thoughtfully arranged sequence.

Detailed Lessons:

Every lesson covers:
- One letter per lesson (shapes of the letter when joining - Beginning, Middle, and End)
- Friendly and unfriendly letters (a detailed parents' and teachers' guide)
- Heavy and light letters (a detailed parents' and teachers' guide)
- The letter with short vowels
- Colours in Arabic
- Shapes in Arabic
- Arabic vocabulary
- Activities on tracing the letters and numbers

Repetitive Learning:

All alphabet lessons are crafted in a repetitive way, explaining short vowels, heavy and light letters, friendly and unfriendly letters, and the shapes of letters at the beginning, middle, and end. This repetition allows sufficient time for students to absorb the basics and implement them easily and effectively.

Alphabet Guide:

The Arabic alphabet in its original order is included at the start and end of this workbook, allowing students to eventually memorise it as a song or through other methods, complementing the series' unique approach. The authors have chosen a unique sequence rather than the traditional alphabetical order, allowing students to effectively recognise each letter individually without referring to the alphabetical song. Each of the 7 letters is carefully selected and introduced in groups or individually, depending on the similarities in letters' shapes, sounds, and characteristics.

دليل للآباء والمعلمين

افتح باب تعلم اللغة العربية مع طفلك أو تلميذك من خلال هذا الكتاب المليء بالتمارين الممتعة والرسومات الزاهية! يجعل هذا الكتاب تعلم اللغة العربية مغامرة مثيرة.

ما بداخل الكتاب :

هذا الكتاب هو جزء من سلسلة "أحب العربية – المرحلة الابتدائية"، والتي قامت بنشرها شركة Arabic Joyride Press . إنه الجزء الأول ويغطي الحروف السبعة الأولى من اللغة العربية. يتم تقديم كل حرف كدرس فردي بترتيب مدروس

كل درس يشمل الآتي

- حرفًا واحدًا لكل درس (أشكال الحرف عند التوصيل – البداية، الوسط، والنهاية)
- الحروف المتعاونة وغير المتعاونة (دليل مفصل للآباء و المعلمين)
- الحروف المفخمة و المرققة (دليل مفصل للآباء و المعلمين)
- الحرف مع الحركات القصيرة
- المفردات العربية
- أنشطة على ممارسة كتابة الحروف و الأرقام
- الأشكال بالعربية
- الألوان بالعربية

التعلم التكراري

تم تصميم دروس الحروف بطريقة تكرارية، تشرح الحركات القصيرة، الحروف المفخمة و المرققة، الحروف المتعاونة و غير المتعاونة وأشكال الحروف في البداية و الوسط والنهاية . هذا التكرار يسمح للطلاب باستوعاب أساسيات اللغة العربية وتنفيذها بسهولة وفعالية

دليل الحروف الأبجدية

تشمل الحروف الأبجدية العربية بترتيبها الأصلي في بداية ونهاية هذا الكتاب، مما يسمح للطلاب في النهاية بحفظها كأغنية أو من خلال طرق أخرى، مكملة نهج السلسلة الفريد . اختار المؤلفون ترتيبًا فريدًا بدلاً من الترتيب الأبجدي التقليدي، مما يسمح للطلاب بالتعرف على كل حرف بشكل فعال دون الرجوع إلى الأغنية الأبجدية. تم اختيار كل من الحروف بعناية وتقديمها في مجموعات أو بشكل فردي، اعتمادًا على تشابهات أشكال وأصوات وخصائص الحروف

Kindergarten - Part one

Why This Book?

- **Quick and Easy Learning:** Designed to help your child or student recognise the Arabic alphabet with short and long vowels quickly.
- **Fun and Interactive:** Every lesson is structured to be enjoyable and easy to understand.
- **Versatile Use:** Perfect for home learning and school settings. Each lesson includes a homework page for reinforced learning.

Give your child or student a head start in Arabic with this carefully crafted guide that makes learning Arabic a delightful experience!

Important Notes to Consider

Introduction of Letters
In this book series, when explaining each letter, the letters are introduced as they are pronounced with the short vowel Fat-hah and not by their original names. The authors believe this method is better for children at this age to start learning the sound of each letter before learning its name. This approach helps them read words more accurately.

Reference to Original Names:
All alphabets' original names are introduced in order at the beginning of this book for reference.

Special Note on Letters Pronunciation:
It is important to note that the letters ح (Ha) and خ (Kha), which are part of the lessons mentioned in this workbook, do not resemble any letter in English in terms of pronunciation.

To indicate this distinction:
- A line is placed on top of the letter ح (Ha).
- A line is placed under the letter خ (Kha).

لماذا هذا الكتاب؟

تعلم سريع وسهل: مصمم لمساعدة طفلك أو طالبك على التعرف على الحروف الأبجدية العربية مع الحركات القصيرة والمدود بسرعة

مرح وتفاعلي: كل درس مصمم ليكون ممتعًا وسهل الفهم

استخدام متعدد: مثالي للتعلم في المنزل والمدارس. كل درس يتضمن صفحة للواجبات لتعزيز التعلم

امنح طفلك أو طالبك بداية قوية في اللغة العربية مع هذا الدليل المصمم بعناية والذي يجعل تعلم اللغة العربية تجربة ممتعة!

ملاحظات هامة يجب مراعاتها

تقديم الحروف
في هذه السلسلة من الكتب، يتم تقديم الحروف عند شرح كل حرف كما يُنطق بالحركة القصيرة الفتحة وليس بأسمائها الأصلية. يعتقد المؤلفون أن هذه الطريقة أفضل للأطفال في هذا العمر ليبدأوا بتعلم صوت كل حرف قبل تعلم اسمه. هذه الطريقة تساعدهم على قراءة الكلمات بدقة أكبر

الإشارة إلى الأسماء الأصلية للحروف الأبجدية
تُعرض أسماء الحروف الأبجدية الأصلية بالترتيب في بداية هذا الكتاب كمرجع

ملاحظة خاصة حول نطق الحروف
من المهم ملاحظة أن الحرفين ح و خ، اللذان هما جزء من الدروس المذكورة في هذا الكتاب، لا يشبهان أي حرف في اللغة الإنجليزية من حيث النطق

للإشارة إلى هذا الفرق، عند كتابتهما باللغة الإنجليزية:

- تم وضع خط فوق الحرف ح (Ha)
- تم وضع خط تحت الحرف خ (Kha)

A Message From The Author

What inspired me to embark on the journey of writing and publishing this Arabic workbook series is my deep and enduring connection with the Arabic language, cultivated since my teenage years in Kuwait. Immersing myself in this rich language and its endless nuances deepened my love for the Quran. I began sharing this knowledge with my family and those around me, following the teachings of the Prophet Muhammad (PBUH). As my children grew and started families of their own, I taught my grandchildren the importance of preserving their mother tongue, the sacred language of the Quran, recognising that translations can never fully capture the essence of Allah's words.

Over the years, I witnessed firsthand how Muslims in the West struggled with maintaining their connection to the Arabic language, which often compromised their spiritual engagement with the Quran. In my opinion, this is largely due to the inadequacies of existing curricula in Arabic institutions in Australia. These programmes either underestimated students' capacity to learn Arabic quickly or overwhelmed them with overseas syllabi that were not tailored to the needs of bilingual students from non-native Arabic backgrounds.

This workbook series is designed to bridge that gap. It provides a comprehensive and practical approach to learning Arabic, guiding students from basic dialects to Arabic Fus-ha, enabling them to read and understand the Quran fluently. Importantly, this series is inclusive, catering to students of all linguistic and religious backgrounds. I am honoured to support students worldwide in beginning their Arabic language journey.

May Allah SWT bless my sincere efforts and accept this work as Sadaqah Jariyah for my parents, my husband and his parents, my children, my students, and the broader Muslim community. Ameen.

Sincerely,

Widad Salman

رسالة من المؤلفة

ما ألهمني لبدء رحلة كتابة ونشر هذه السلسلة من الكتب هو اتصالي العميق والدائم باللغة العربية الذي تم تطويره منذ سنوات مراهقتي في الكويت. غمرت نفسي في هذه اللغة الغنية وتفاصيلها التي لا تنتهي مما عمق حبي للقرآن الكريم. بدأت بمشاركة هذه المعرفة مع عائلتي ومن حولي، متبعةً تعاليم النبي محمد (صلى الله عليه وسلم). عندما كبر أطفالي وبدأوا في تكوين أسرهم الخاصة، علمت أحفادي أهمية الحفاظ على لغتهم الأم، لغة القرآن المقدسة، مدركةً أن الترجمات لا يمكن أن تنقل جوهر كلام الله بشكل كامل.

على مر السنين، شهدت بنفسي كيف كافح المسلمون في الغرب للحفاظ على اتصالهم باللغة العربية، مما أثر غالبًا على ارتباطهم الروحي بالقرآن. في رأيي، يعود ذلك بشكل كبير إلى القصور في المناهج الحالية في المؤسسات العربية وتحديدا في أستراليا كوني أعيش فيها. فإما أن تقلل هذه البرامج من قدرة الطلاب على تعلم اللغة العربية بسرعة، أو تطغى عليهم بالمناهج الخارجية التي لم تكن مصممة لتلبية احتياجات الطلاب ثنائيي اللغة من خلفيات غير ناطقة بالعربية.

تم تصميم سلسلة كتب النشاط هذه لسد تلك الفجوة. فهي توفر نهجًا شاملاً وعمليًا لتعلم اللغة العربية، مما يوفر للطلاب تعلم أساسيات اللغة العربية أولا و من ثم انتقالهم لتعلم اللغة العربية الفصحى بشكل فعال، مما يمكنهم من قراءة القرآن وفهمه بطلاقة. الأهم من ذلك، أن هذه السلسلة شاملة، وتلبي احتياجات الطلاب من جميع الخلفيات اللغوية والدينية. يشرفني دعم الطلاب في جميع أنحاء العالم في بدء رحلتهم في تعلم اللغة العربية.

أسأل الله سبحانه وتعالى أن يبارك في جهودي المخلصة ويتقبل هذا العمل كصدقة جارية لوالدي وزوجي ووالديه وأطفالي وطلابي والمجتمع المسلم الأوسع. آمين.

المخلصة
وداد سلمان

Student information

 My name : ....

.... : اِسْمِي

 My teacher : ....

.... : مُعَلِّمَتِي

The Alphabet

 Alif أ	 Baa' ب	 Taa' ت	 Thaa' ث
 Jeem ج	 Ḥaa' ح	 Khaa' خ	 Daal د
 Thaal ذ	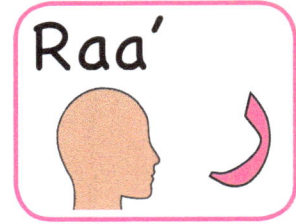 Raa' ر	 Zaay ز	 Seen س
 Sheen ش	 Saad ص	 Dhaad ض	 Taa' ط
 Thaa' ظ	 Āyn ع	 Ghayn غ	 Faa' ف
 Qaaf ق	 Kaaf ك	 Laam ل	 Meem م
 Noon ن	 Haa' ه	 Waaw و	 Yaa' ي

© Arabic Joyride Press

Introducing the characters

Assalamu Alaikum....

My name is Nahool !
In this workbook, we will take you on a fun journey with 7 Arabic letters!

Assalamu Alaikum....

My name is Nahlah !
Open the next page to meet the first letter ح !

© Arabic Joyride Press

Lesson 1 : ح 🔊 H̄a

Horse

حِصَانْ   🔊   H̄i̱saan

Remember

ح Is a light and a friendly letter

أ ب ت ث ج خ د ذ ر ز س ش ص ض ط ظ ع غ ف ق ك ل م ن هـ و ي

 Trace letter Ḥa حَ خَطِّطْ الْحَرْفْ

*Start writing from the right

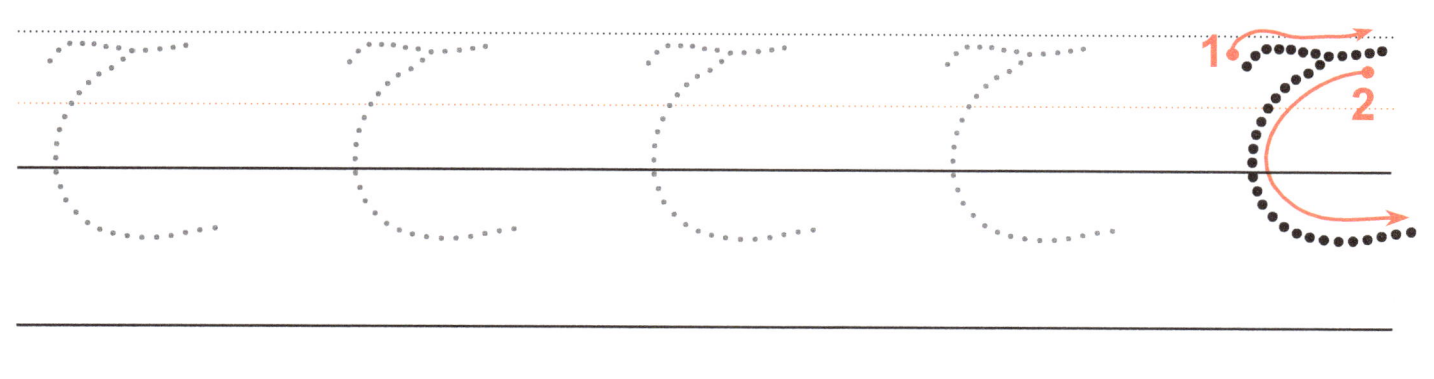

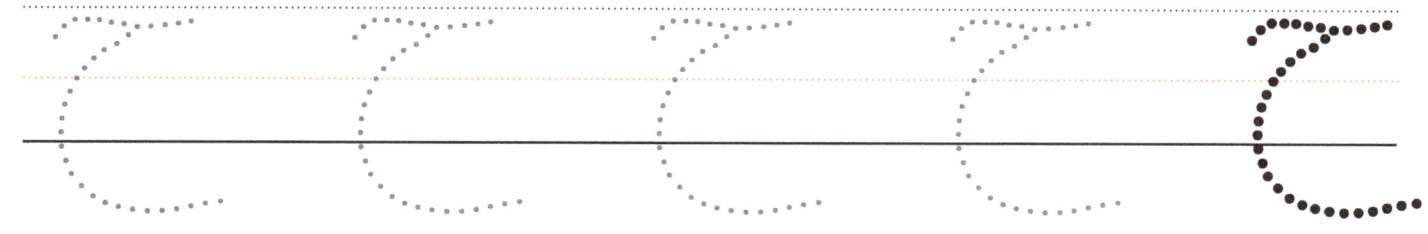

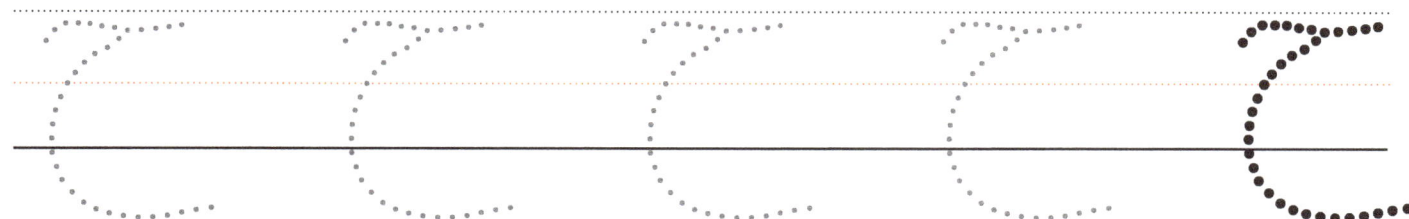

Color letter ح at the beginning of each word aḥmar.

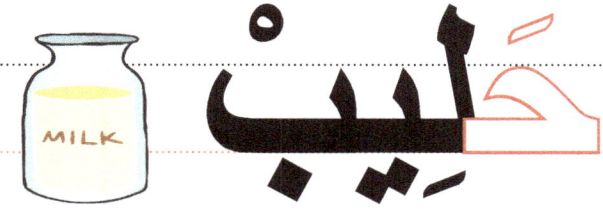 

5

© Arabic Joyride Press

Parets'/Teachers' guide to explaining friendly letters

Friendly letters are letters that can join other letters from both sides (back and front)!

They join by holding hands!

There are 22 friendly letters:

ب ت ث ج ح خ س ش ص ض ط ظ ع غ ف ق ك ل م ن ه و ي

The Letter ح is a friendly letter. Look how it holds hands from both sides when joining in the middle of a word:

Now look how the letter ح gives only one hand from the front when it joins at the beginning of a word:

And finally, look how the letter ح gives only one hand from the back when joining at the end of a word:

© Arabic Joyride Press

Parets'/Teachers' guide to explaining light and heavy letters

There are two types of letters based on pronunciation: (Heavy letters and Light letters).

Heavy letters are letters that are pronouced more heavily and they require more effort to pronounce compared to light letters!

There are Seven Heavy letters:

خ - ص - ض - غ - ط - ق - ظ

The rest of the letters are light:

أ-ب-ت-ث-ج-ح-د-ذ-ر-ز-س-ش-ع-ف-ل-م-ن-ه-و-ي-ك

Heavy letters:

Light letters:

© Arabic Joyride Press

The shapes of Ḥa ح when joining

Letter Ḥa can change dresses when joining other letters at the:

| End | Middle | Beginning |

Color letter Ḥa dresses :
at the beginning aḥmar, in the middle aṣfar
and at the end azraq.

تَحْتْ   حَلْقْ   مِلْحْ

8

Introducing short vowels with letter Ḥa ح

There are four short vowels. They are called (Ḥarakaat) (حَرَكَاتْ)

They are symbols (́ ُ ْ ِ) that can sit on top or under letters. (́) is called Fat-hah, (ُ) is called Dammah and (ْ) is called Sukoon.

Fat-hah, Dammah and Sukoon can sit only on top of letters.

Imagine them as hats!

(ِ) is called Kasrah, it can sit only under letters.

Imagine Kasrah as a sock!

With Fat-hah	Ḥa	📢	ح
With Dammah	Ḥu	📢	ح
With Sukoon/Silent	Ḥ	📢	ح
With Kasrah	Ḥi	📢	ح

| أ | ب | ت | ث | ج | **ح** | خ | د | ذ | ر | ز | س | ش | ص | ض | ط | ظ | ع | غ | ف | ق | ك | ل | م | ن | هـ | و | ي |

Match letter H̄a ح with its suitable hat or sock.

حَ   حِ   حْ   حُ

 Trace letter H̄a with short vowels.

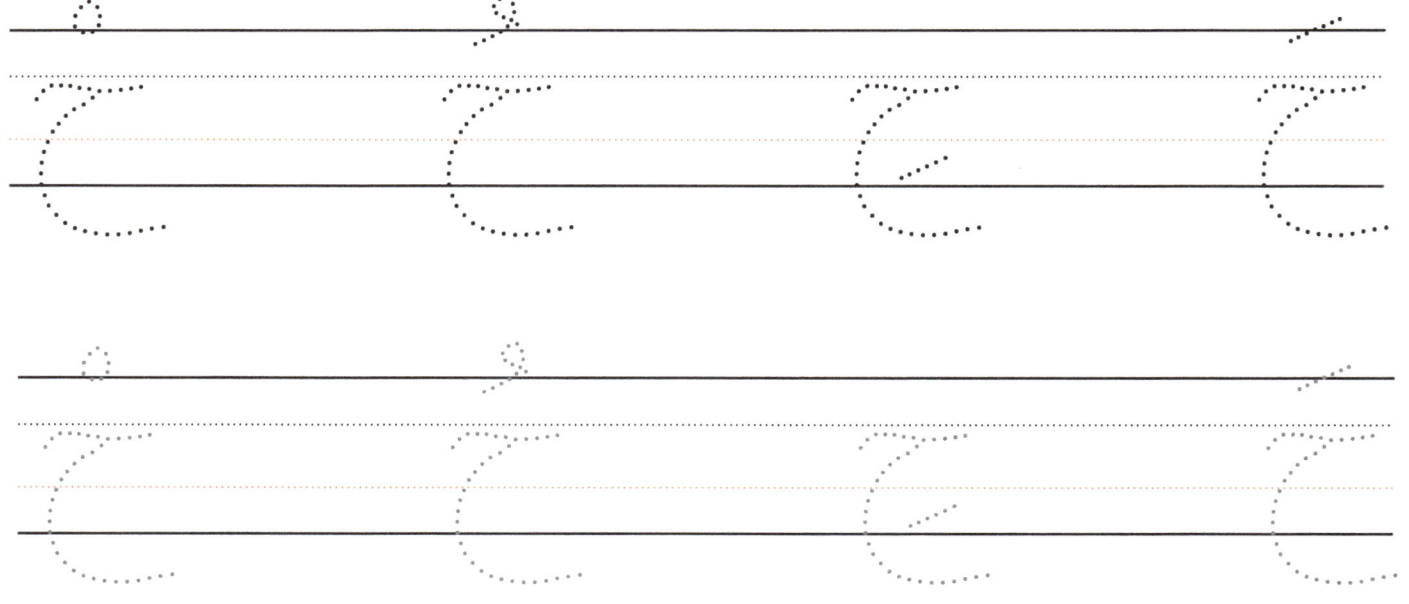

أ ب ت ث ج ح خ د ذ ر ز س ش ص ض ط ظ ع غ ف ق ك ل م ن هـ و ي

Match letter Ḥa with the correct word.

Red   Aḥmar

Chickpeas   Ḥummus

Ḥibr

Ḥab

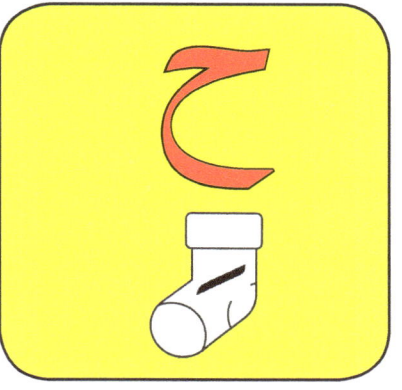

11

© Arabic Joyride Press

 Trace letter Ḥa ح at the beginning, middle and end.

The shapes in Arabic

Circle (Daa'irah - دَائِرَة)

Color all (daa'irah)s a<u>s</u>far and the rest of the shapes azra<u>q</u>.

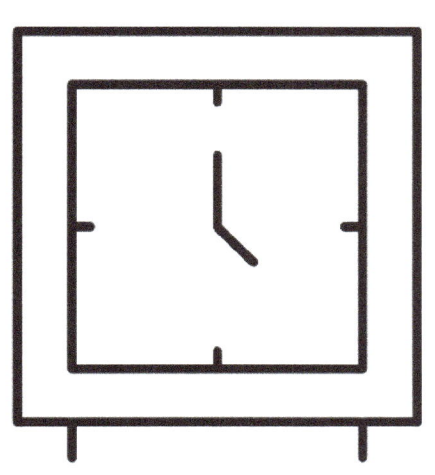

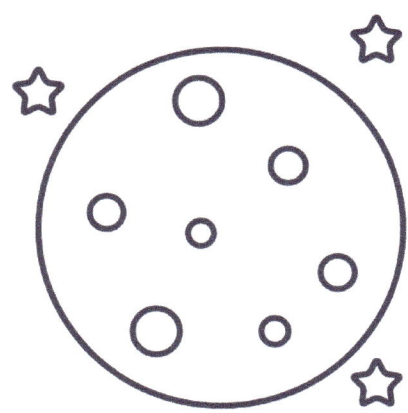

The Arabic numbers

One - Waahid

Zero - Sifr
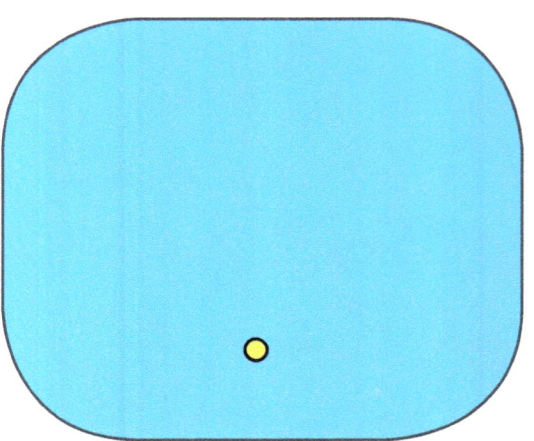

 Trace.

Revision

How many cows (Ba<u>q</u>arah)s can you see in each picture?
Write the Arabic number in the azraq أزرق daa'irah.

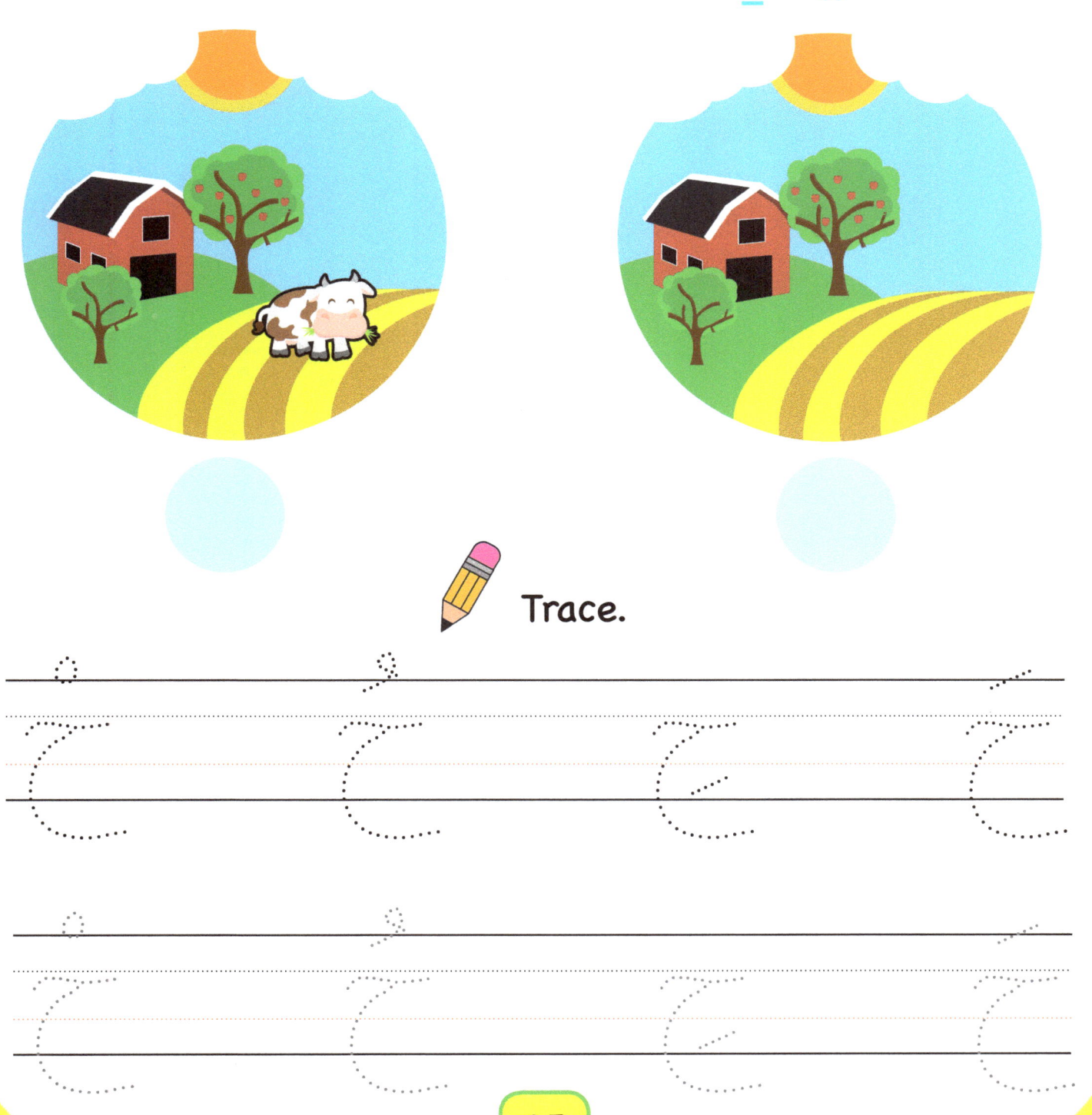

Trace.

Lets write our homework !

Copy letter Ḥa ح inside the dresses.

Beginning

Middle

  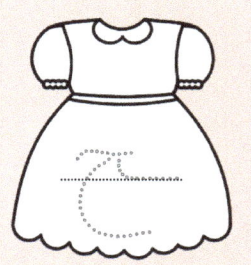 

End

٢٠ ١٩ ١٨ ١٧ ١٦ ١٥ ١٤ ١٣ ١٢ ١١ ١٠ ٩ ٨ ٧ ٦ ٥ ٤ ٣ ٢ ١ ٠

Lets write our homework !

 Copy the numbers.

 Color the daa'irah aḥmar
and the rest of the shapes azraq.

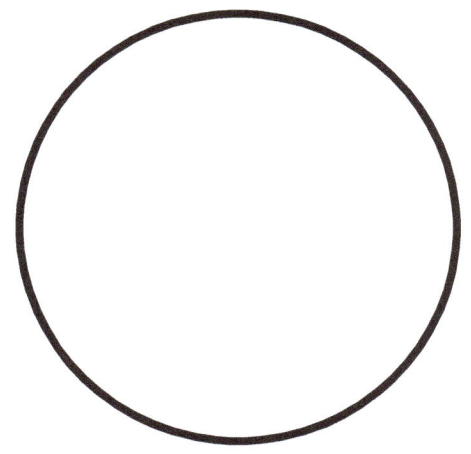
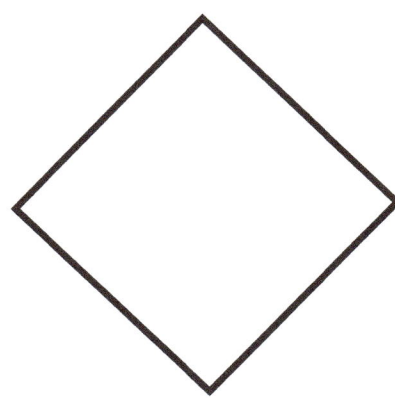

17

© Arabic Joyride Press

Lesson 2: خ Kha

Beetle

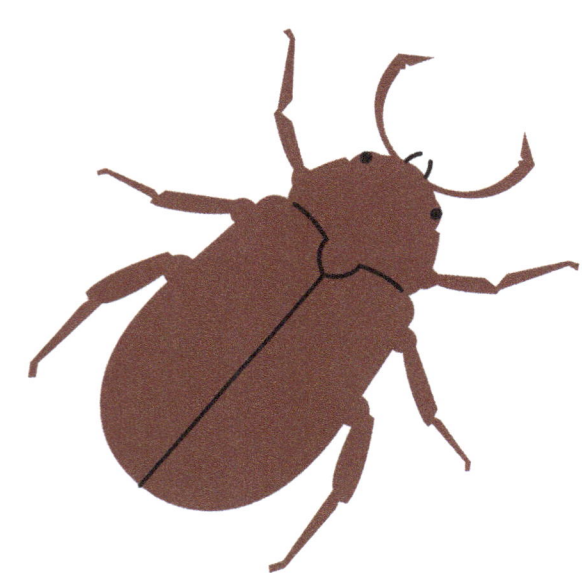

We are sisters!

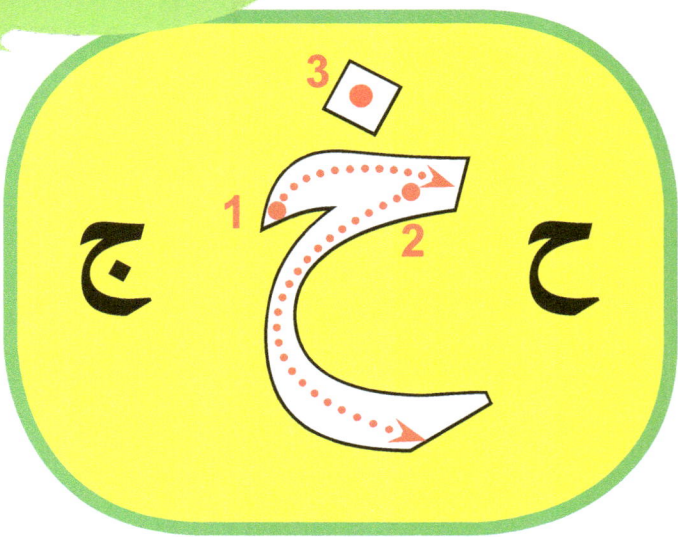

خُنْفُسَاءْ  **Khu**nfusaa'

Remember  خ Is a heavy and a friendly letter

18

أ ب ت ث ج ح خ د ذ ر ز س ش ص ض ط ظ ع غ ف ق ك ل م ن هـ و ي

Trace letter Kha خ خَطِّطْ الحَرْفْ

*Start writing from the right

1 2 3

خ خ خ خ خ

خ خ خ خ خ

خ خ خ خ خ

Color letter خ at the beginning of each word asfar.

 خَسْ

 خَرُوفْ

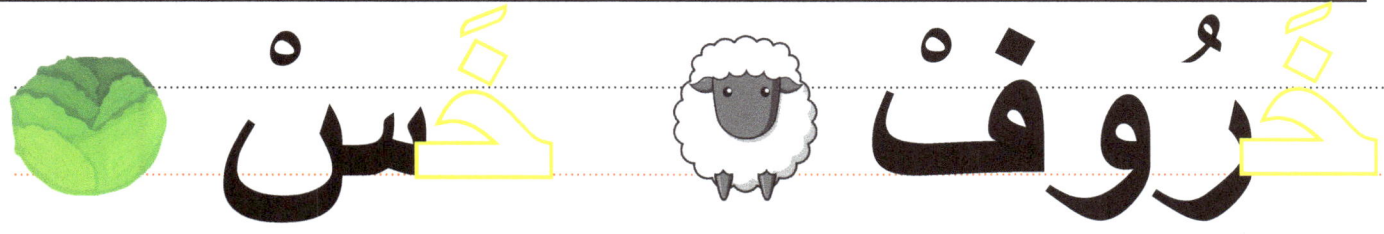

أ ب ت ث ج ح خ د ذ ر ز س ش ص ض ط ظ ع غ ف ق ك ل م ن هـ و ي

The shapes of Kha خ when joining

 letter Kha can change dresses when joining other letters at the:

| End | Middle | Beginning |

Color letter Kha dresses :
at the beginning azraq, in the middle asfar
and at the end ahmar.

خَسْ   بَطِّيخْ   تَخْتْ

20
© Arabic Joyride Press

 letter Kha with short vowels

| With Fat-hah | Kha |  |

| With Dammah | Khu |  |

| With Sukoon/Silent | Kh |  |

| With Kasrah | Khi |  |

Match letter Kha  with its suitable hat or sock.

      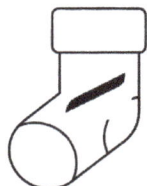   

 Trace letter Kha with short vowels.

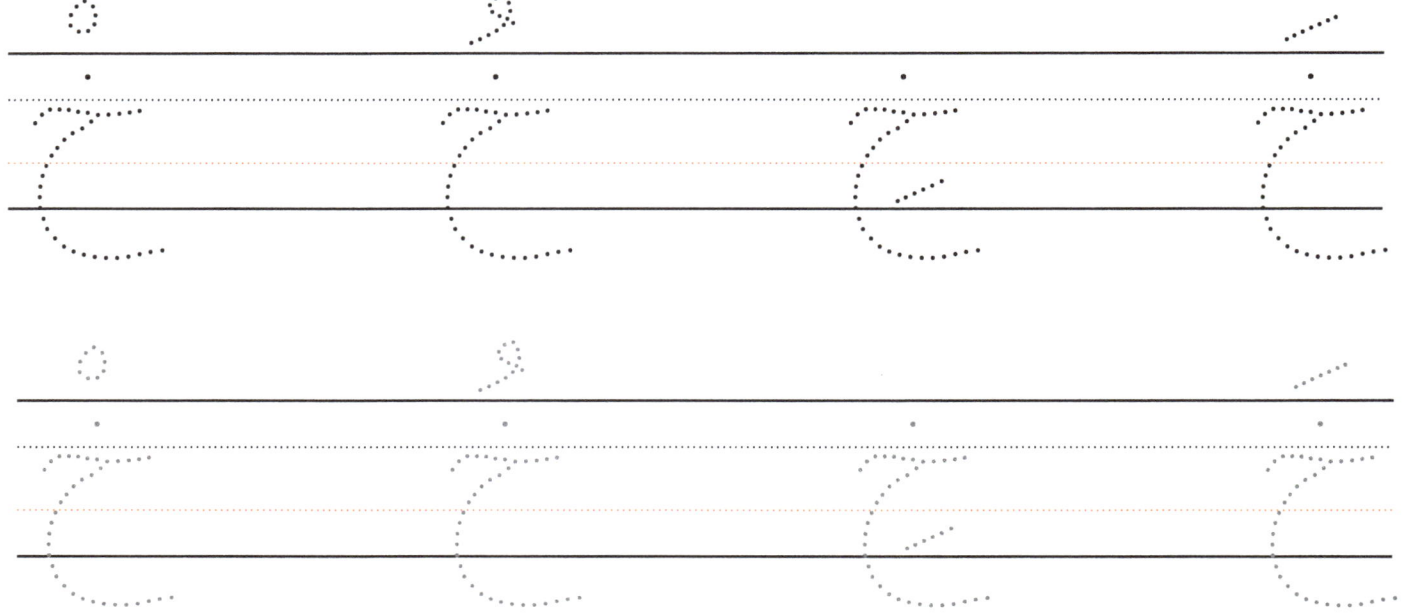

Match letter Kha with the correct word.

Bat — Khuffaash

Chicks — Firaakh

Wood — Khashab

Dagger — Khinjar

Trace letter <u>Kha</u> ﺥ at the beginning, middle and end.

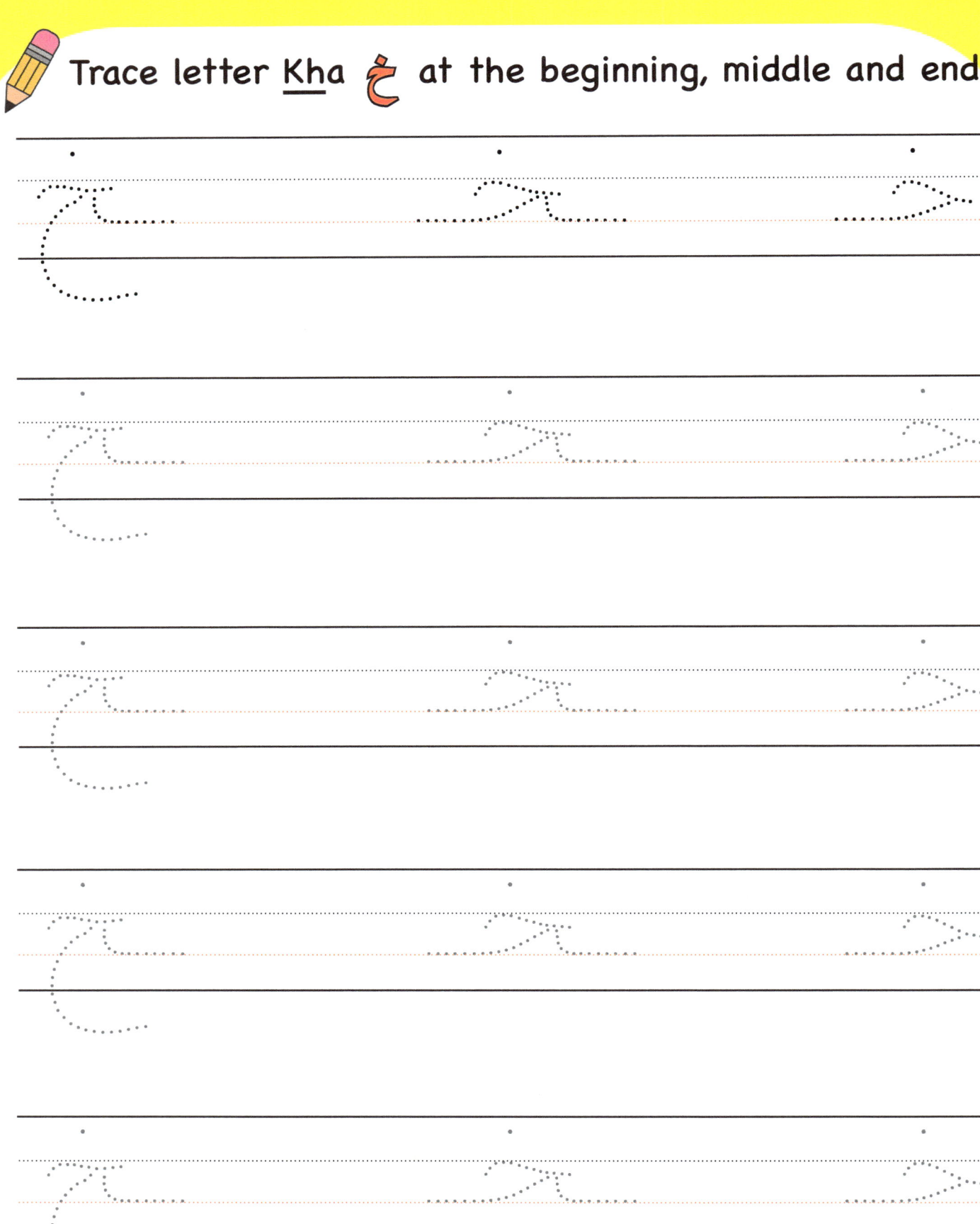

The shapes in Arabic

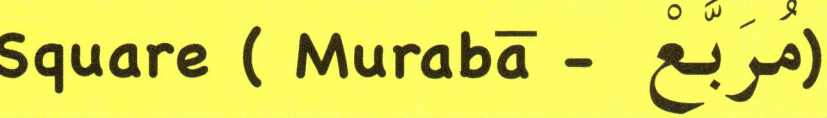

Square (Murabā - مُرَبَّعْ)

Color all (murabā)s **burtuqaaly** and the rest of the shapes **banafsajy**.

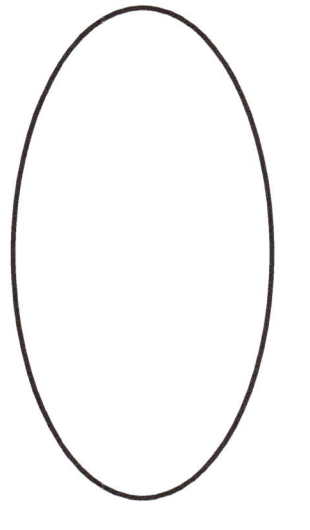

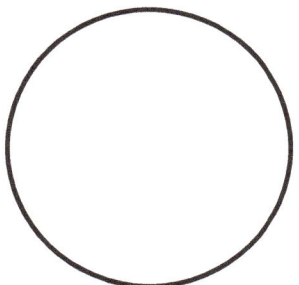
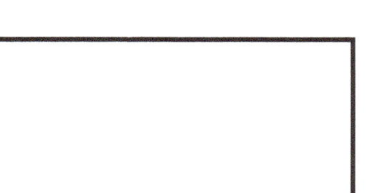

٠ ١ ٢ ٣ ٤ ٥ ٦ ٧ ٨ ٩ ١٠ ١١ ١٢ ١٣ ١٤ ١٥ ١٦ ١٧ ١٨ ١٩ ٢٠

The Arabic numbers

Three - Thalaathah

Two - Ithnaan

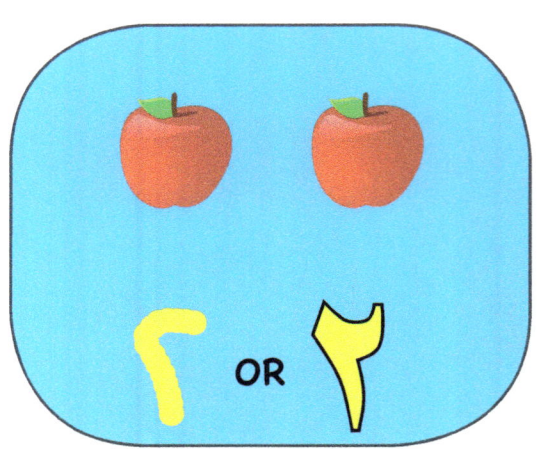

✏️ Trace.

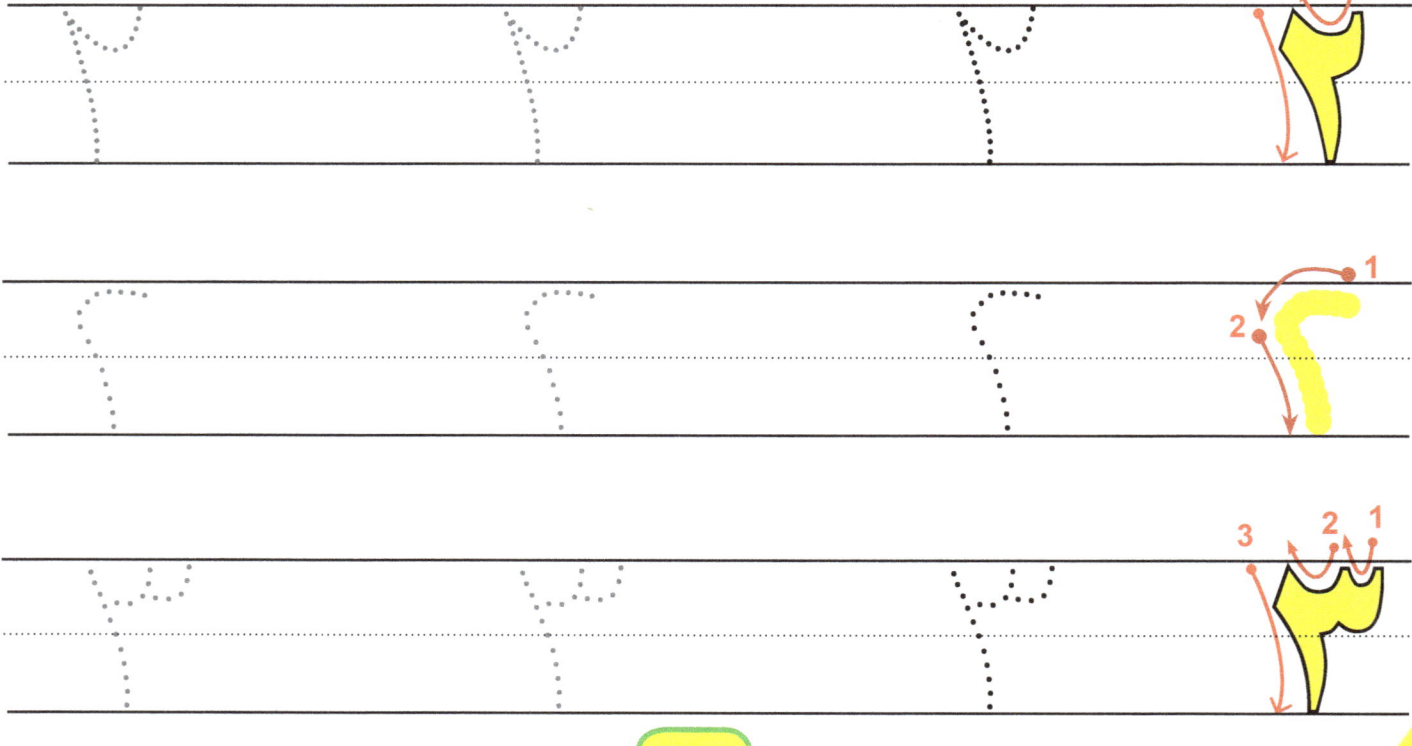

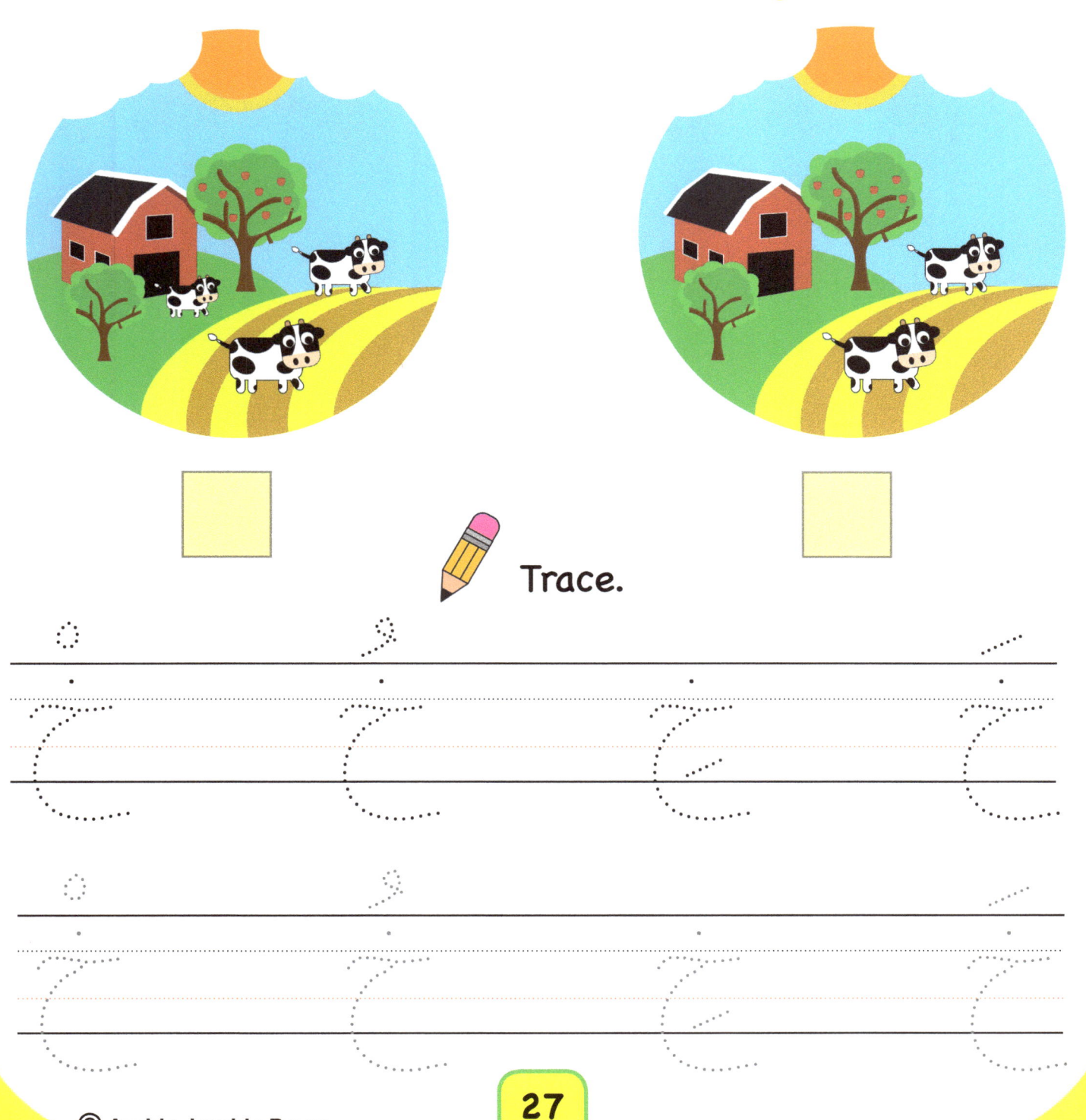

Lets write our homework !

Copy letter Kha  inside the dresses.

Beginning

  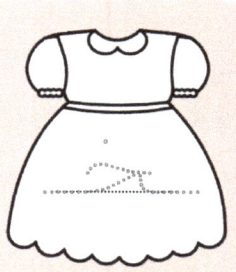 

Middle

  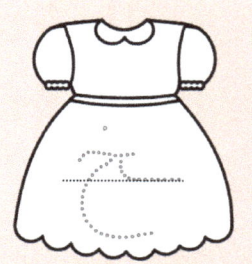 

End

© Arabic Joyride Press

٢٠ ١٩ ١٨ ١٧ ١٦ ١٥ ١٤ ١٣ ١٢ ١١ ١٠ ٩ ٨ ٧ ٦ ٥ ٤ ٣ ٢ ١ ٠

Lets write our homework !

 Copy the numbers.

Color the murabā azraq and the rest of the shapes banafsajy.

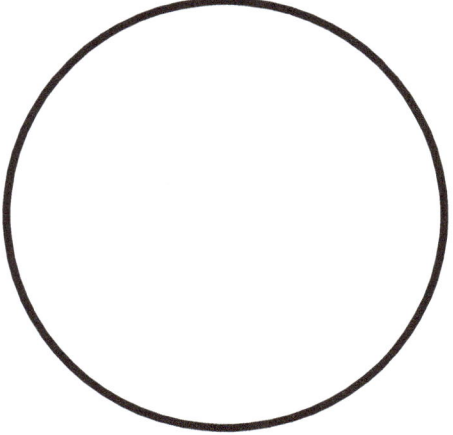

29
© Arabic Joyride Press

Lesson 3 : ج 📢 Ja

Bulldozer

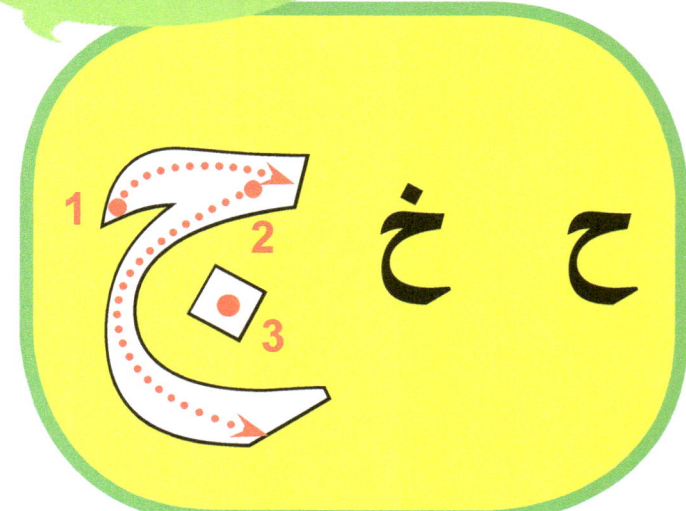

We are sisters!

📢 **Ja**rraafah   جَـرَّافَة

Remember — ج Is a light and a friendly letter

أ ب ت ث ج ح خ د ذ ر ز س ش ص ض ط ظ ع غ ف ق ك ل م ن هـ و ي

 Trace letter Ja   خَطِّطْ الحَرْف ج

*Start writing from the right

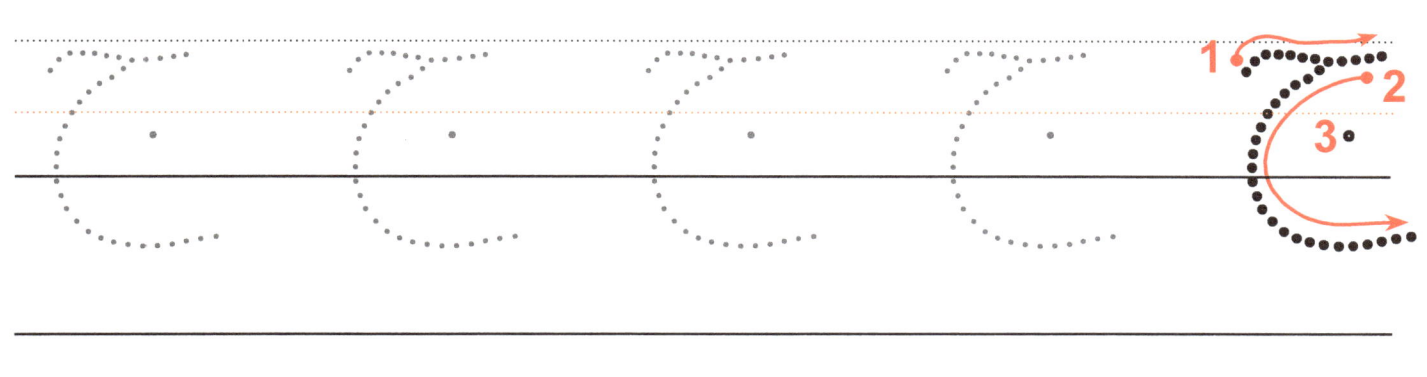

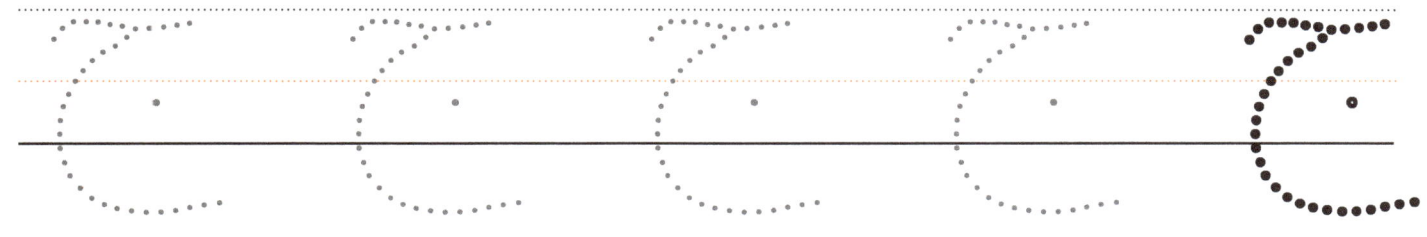

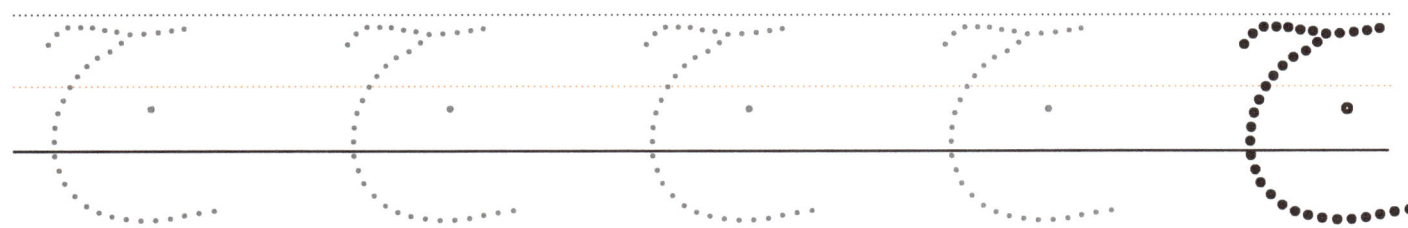

Color letter ج at the beginning of each word *azraq*.

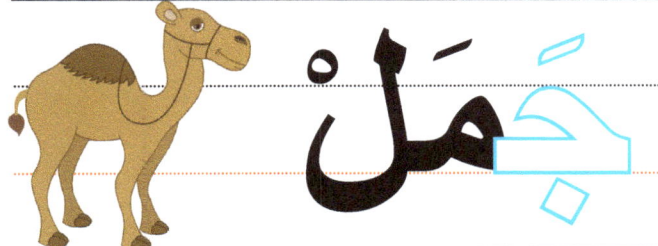

31
© Arabic Joyride Press

The shapes of Ja ج when joining

letter Ja can change dresses when joining other letters at the:

End   Middle   Beginning

Color letter Ja dresses :
at the beginning **banafsajy**, in the middle **akhdar**
and at the end **burtuqaaly**.

فِنْجَان   جَبَلْ   مُهَرِّج

Letter Ja ج with short vowels

| With Fat-hah | Ja | 🔊 | جَ |

| With Dammah | Ju | 🔊 | جُ |

| With Sukoon/Silent | J | 🔊 | جْ |

| With Kasrah | Ji | 🔊 | جِ |

© Arabic Joyride Press

Match letter Ja  with its suitable hat or sock.

 Trace letter Ja with short vowels.

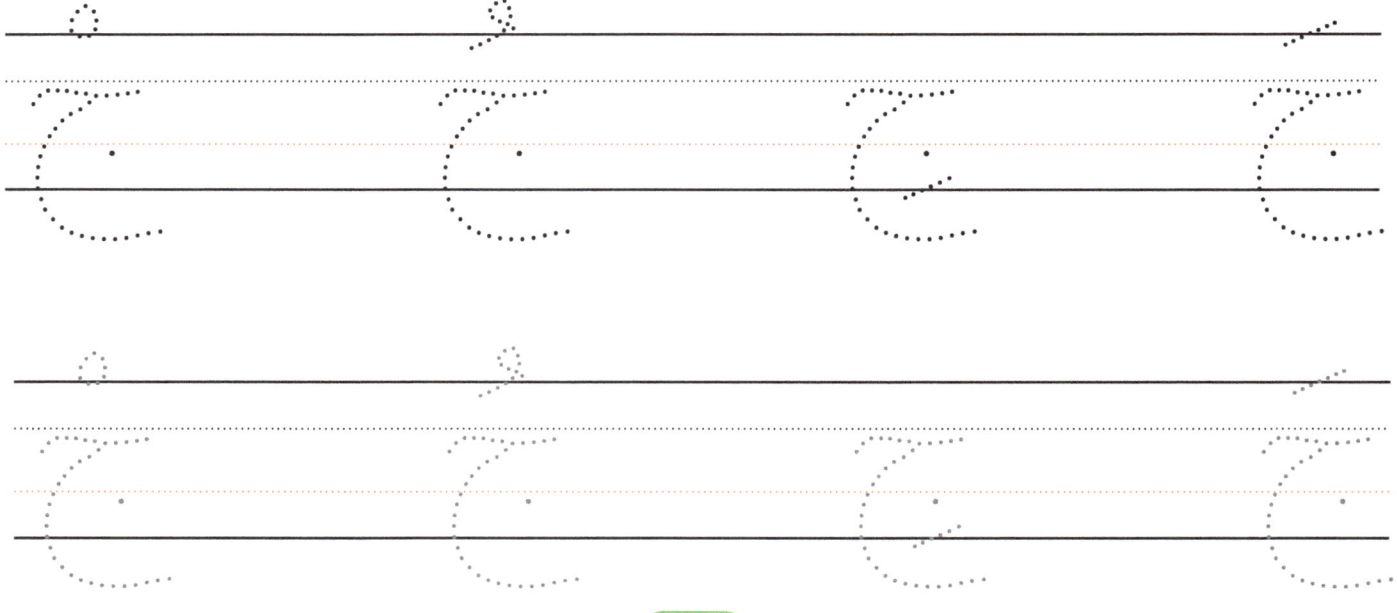

Match letter Ja with the correct word.

جَامُوسْ
Buffalo — Jaamoos

نُجُومْ
Stars — Nujoom

جِسْرْ
Bridge — Jisr

ثَلْجْ
Ice — Thalj

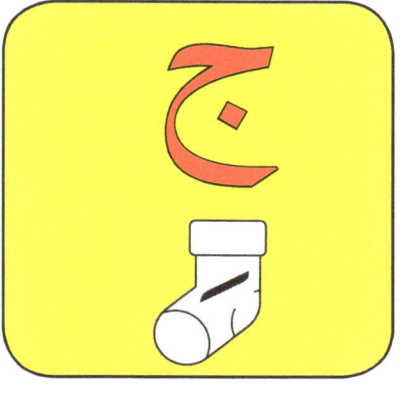

Trace letter Ja ج at the beginning, middle and end.

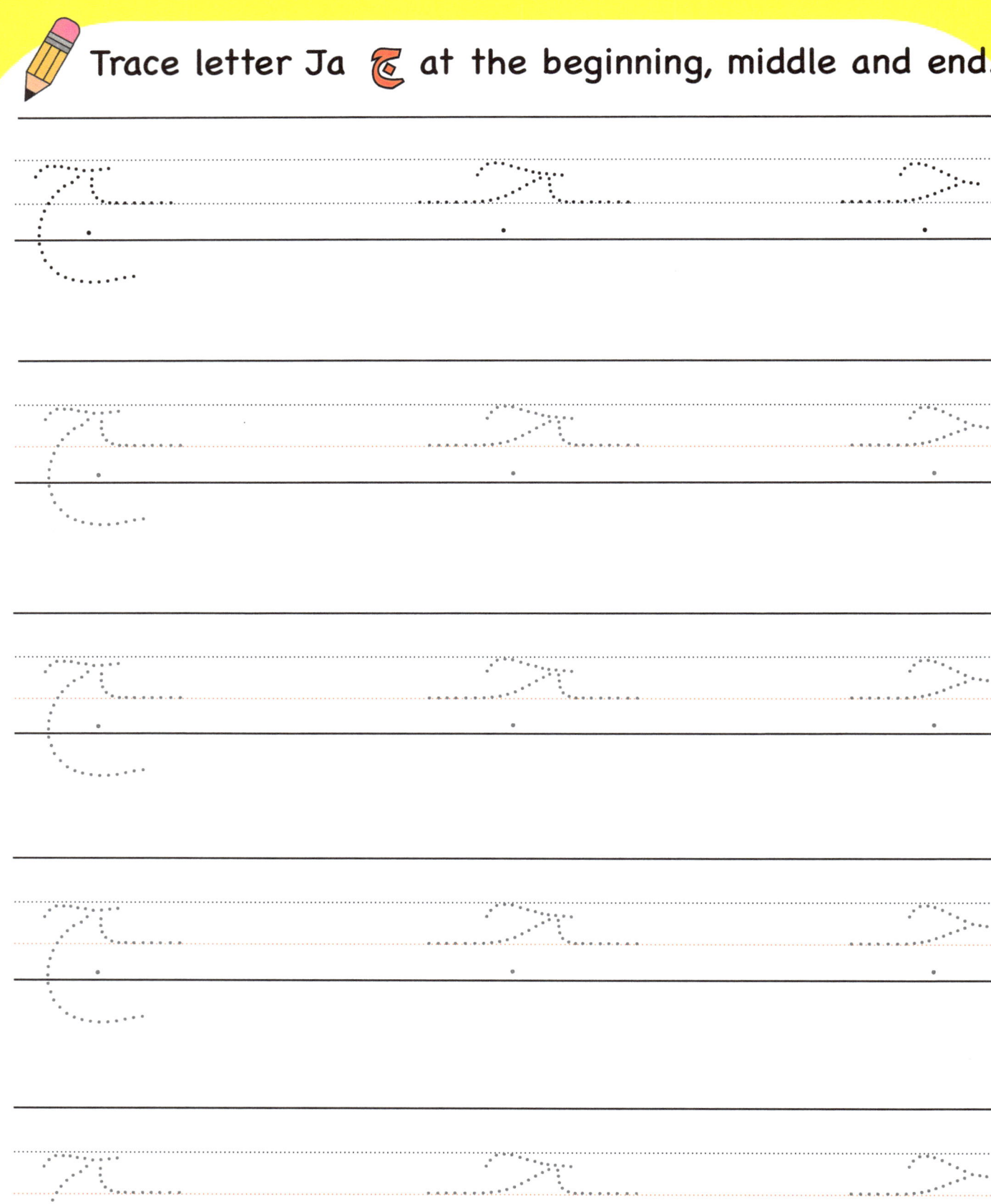

The shapes in Arabic

Rectangle (Mustateel - مُسْتَطِيلْ)

Color all (mustateel)s **asfar**
and the rest of the shapes **banafsajy**.

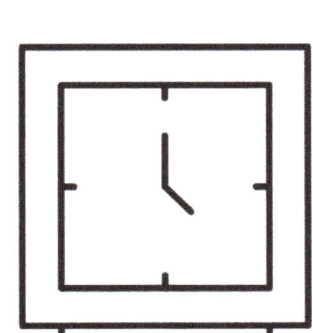

The Arabic numbers

Five - <u>Kh</u>amsah   Four - Arbaāah

 Trace.

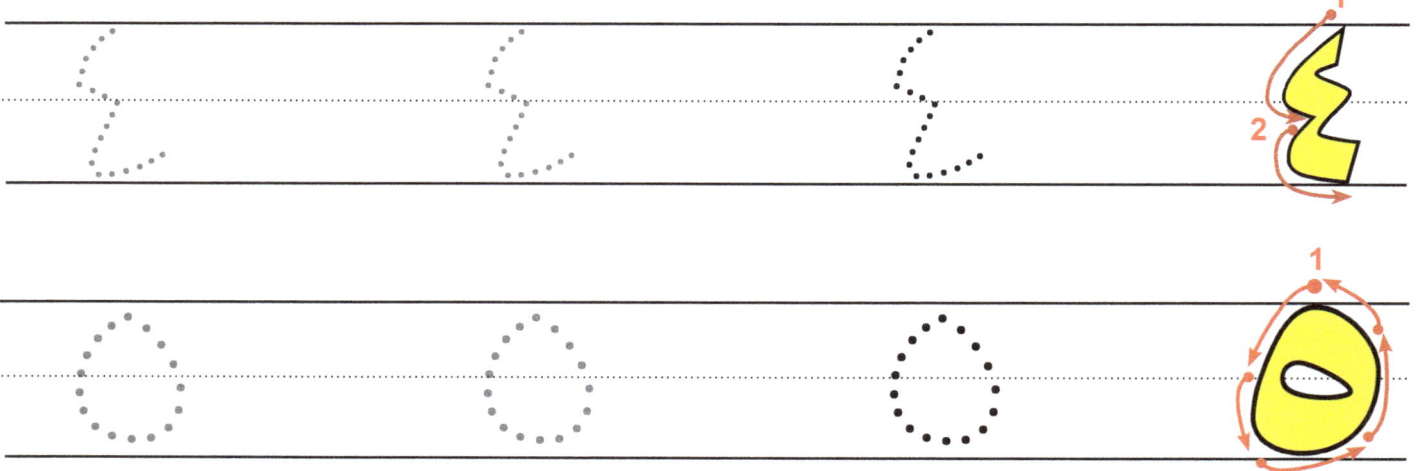

38
© Arabic Joyride Press

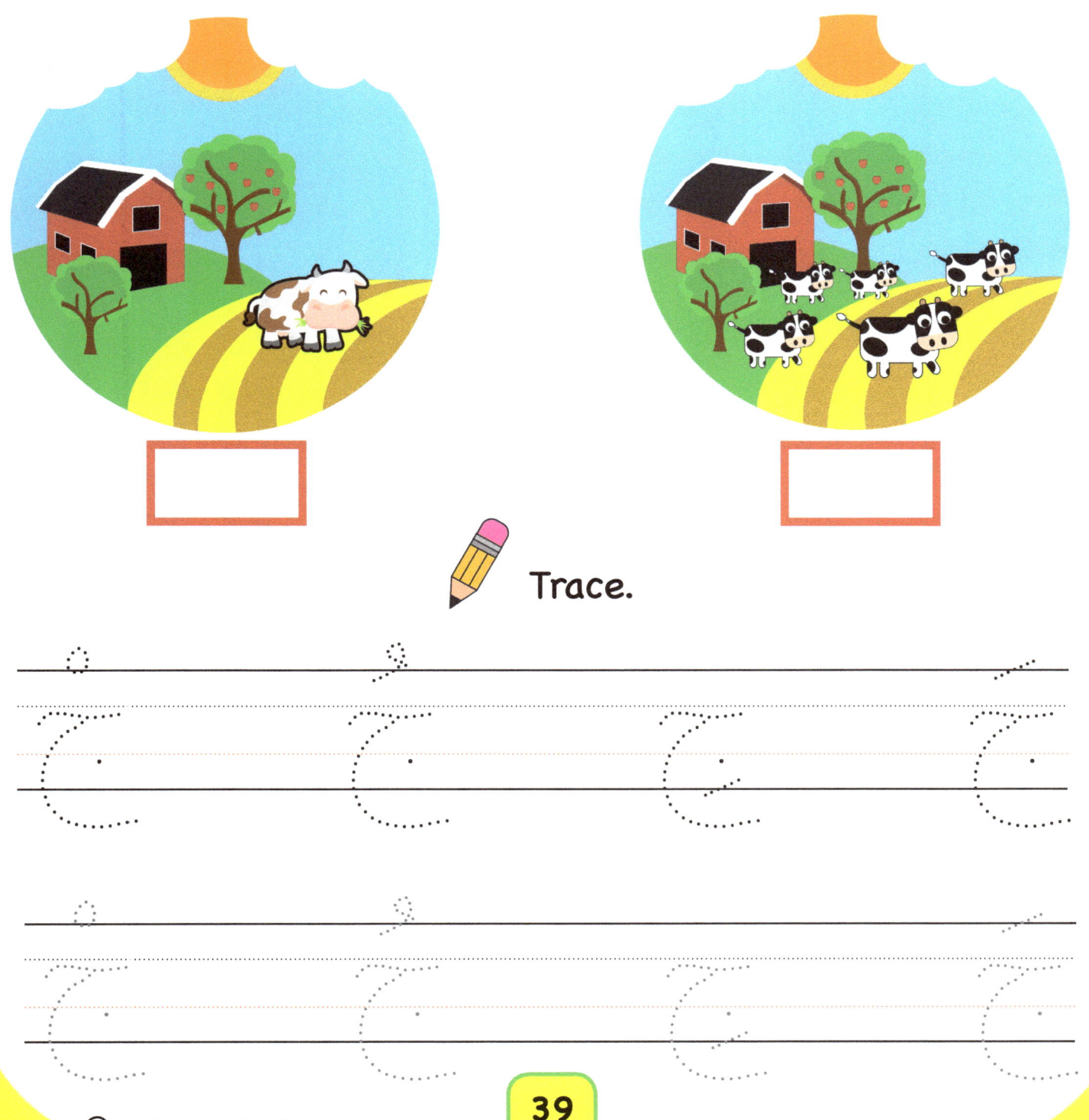

Revision

How many cows (Baqarah)s can you see in each picture? Write the Arabic number in the ahmar أَحْمَرْ mustateel.

Trace.

أ ب ت ث ج ح خ د ذ ر ز س ش ص ض ط ظ ع غ ف ق ك ل م ن هـ و ي

Lets write our homework !

Copy letter Ja inside the dresses.

Beginning

Middle

  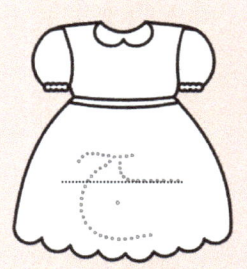 

End

© Arabic Joyride Press

Lets write our homework!

 Copy the numbers.

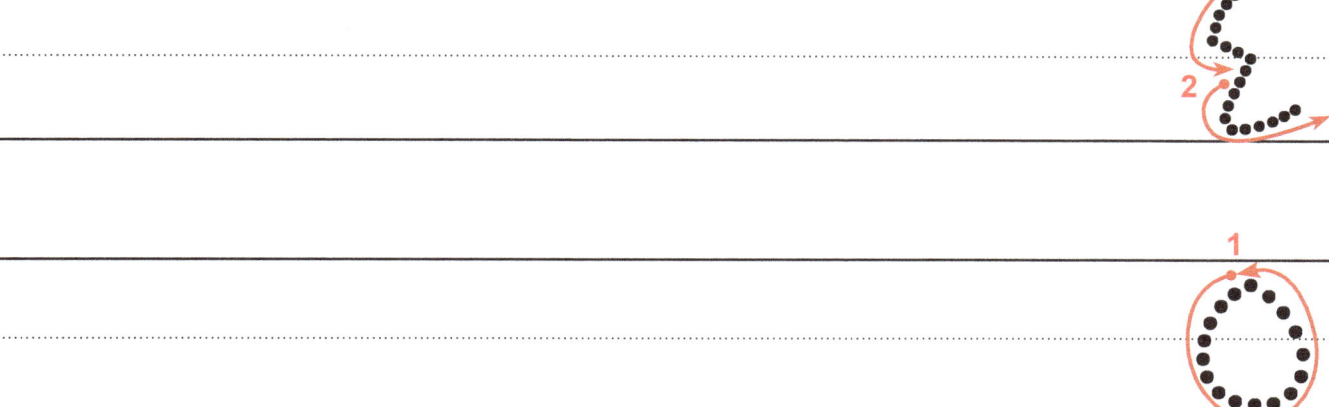

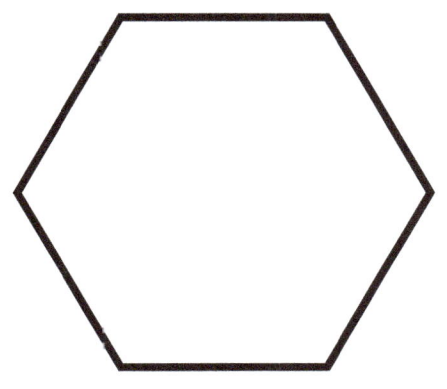 Color the mustateel akhdar and the rest of the shapes banafsajy.

Parets'/Teachers' guide to explaining unfriendly letters

Unfriendly letters are letters that can join other letters only from the back. They join by holdin hands. There are seven unfriendly letters:

Letter أ is an unfriendly letter, look how it only holds one hand from the back when joining in the middle of a word:

Parets'/Teachers' guide to explaining unfriendly letters

Now look how letter أ is not holding hands from the front when it comes at the beginning of a word:

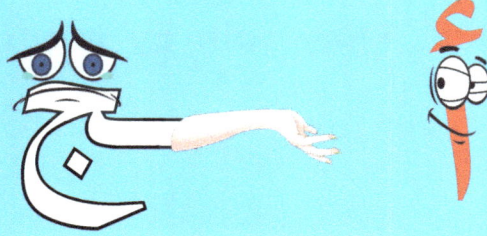

And finally, look how letter أ gives only one hand from the back when joining at the end of a word:

© Arabic Joyride Press

Lesson 4 : أ  A'a

Rabbit

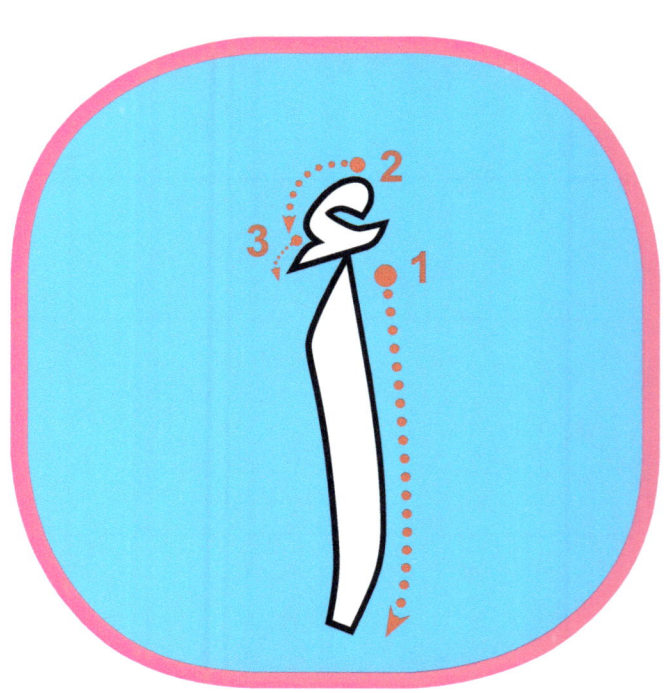

أَرْنَبْ  A'rnab

 Is a light and an unfriendly letter!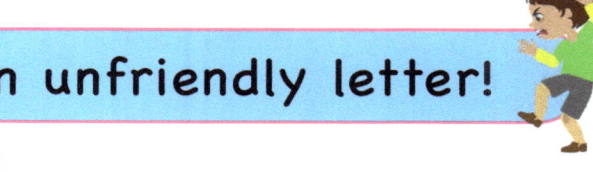

44
© Arabic Joyride Press

أ ب ت ث ج ح خ د ذ ر ز س ش ص ض ط ظ ع غ ف ق ك ل م ن هـ و ي

 Trace letter A'a   أ   خَطِّطْ الحَرْفْ

*Start writing from the right

Color letter أ at the beginning of each word Akhdar.

45

© Arabic Joyride Press

أ ب ت ث ج ح خ د ذ ر ز س ش ص ض ط ظ ع غ ف ق ك ل م ن هـ و ي

The shapes of A'a أ when joining

letter A'a can change dresses when joining other letters at the:

| End | Middle | Beginning |

Color letter A'a dresses :
at the beginning **burtuqaaly**, in the middle **aḥmar** and at the end **azraq**.

مَلْجَأْ

أَكَلَ

يَأْكُلْ

46
© Arabic Joyride Press

letter A'a ا with short vowels

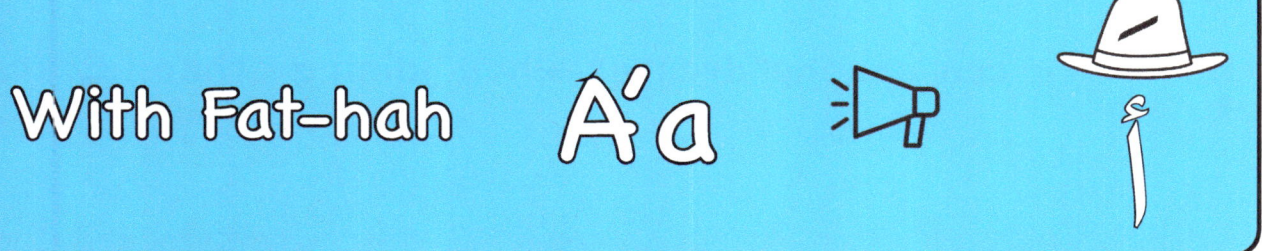

With Fat-hah — A'a — أ

With Dammah — U' — أ

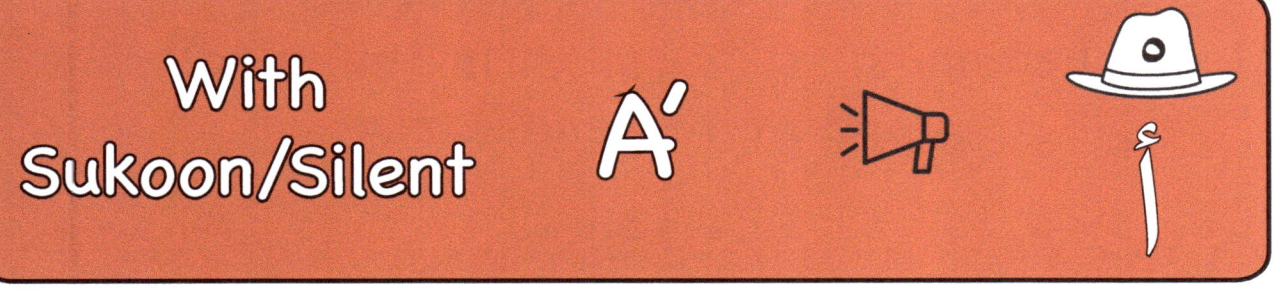

With Sukoon/Silent — A' — أْ

With Kasrah — E — إ

Match letter A'a أ with its suitable hat or sock.

أْ   أَ   إِ   أُ

Trace letter A'a with short vowels.

Match letter A'a with the correct word.

كَأْسْ
Cup — Ka's

إِبْرِيقْ
Pot — I'breeq

أَرْنَبْ
Rabbit — A'arnab

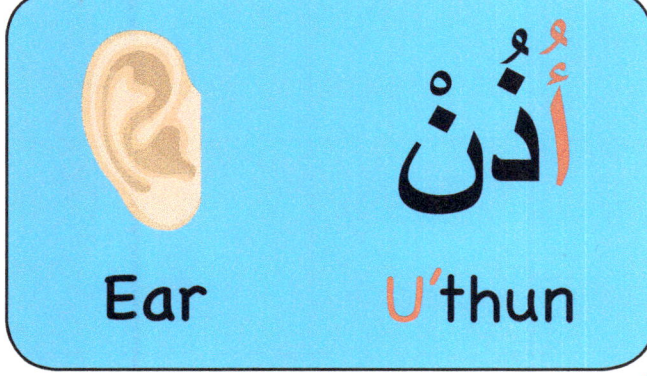

أُذُنْ
Ear — U'thun

Trace letter A'a ﺍ at the beginning, middle and end.

The shapes in Arabic

Triangle (Muthallath - مُثَلَّثٌ)

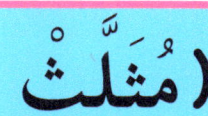
Color all (muthallath)s **zahry**
and the rest of the shapes **azraq**.

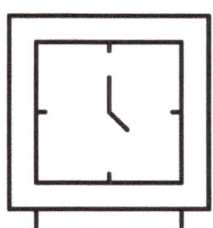

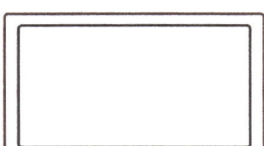

The Arabic numbers

Seven - Sabāah

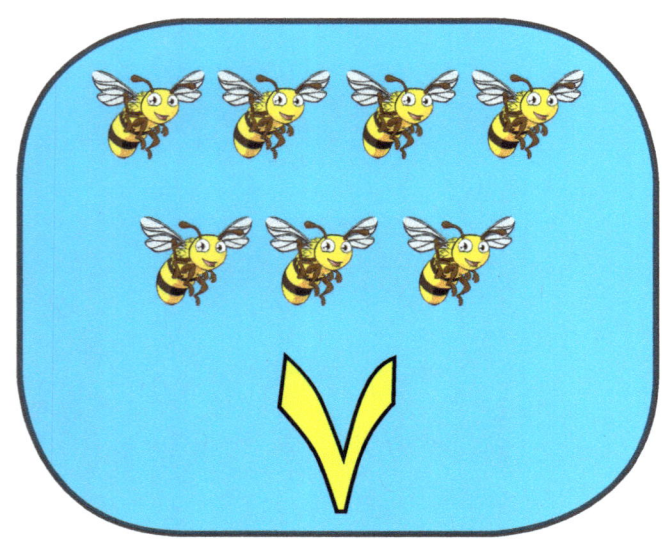

Six - Sittah

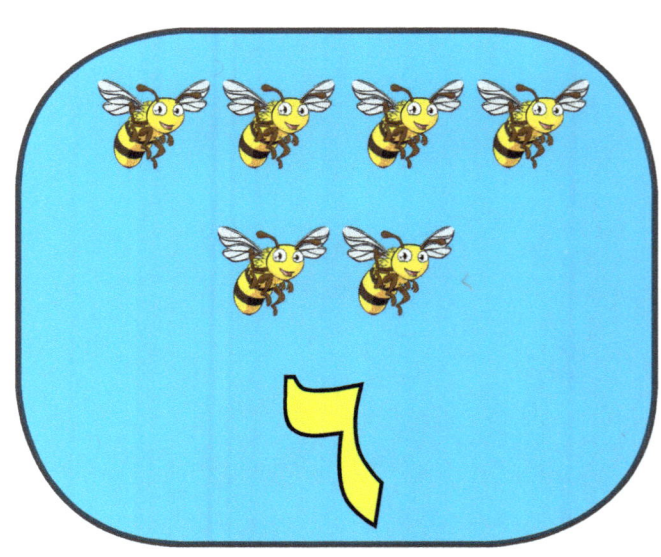

 Trace.

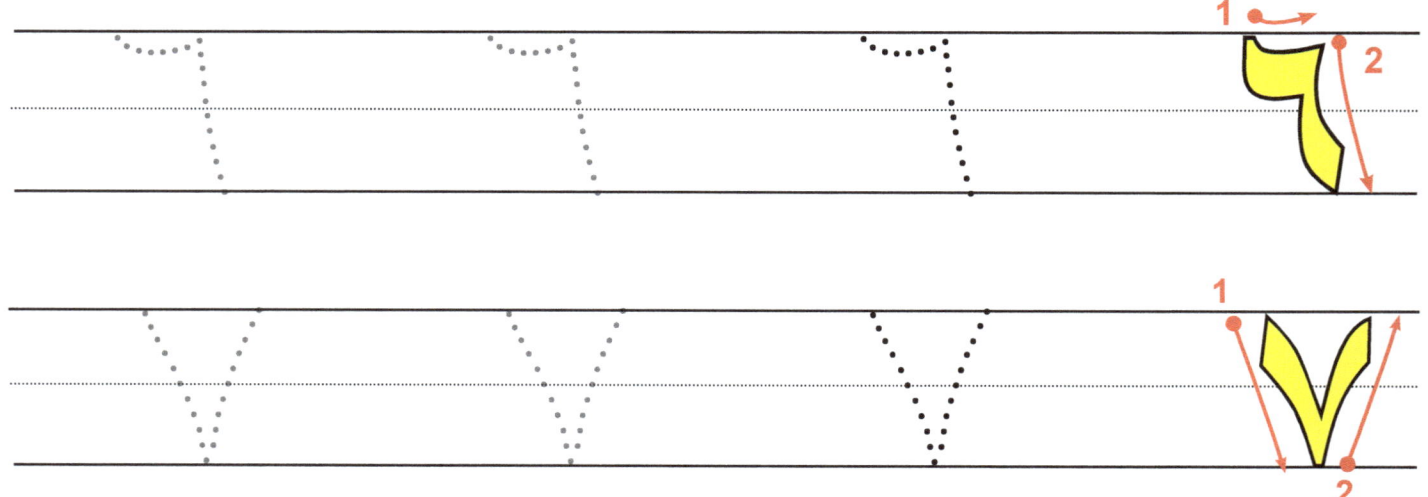

أ ب ت ث ج ح خ د ذ ر ز س ش ص ض ط ظ ع غ ف ق ك ل م ن هـ و ي

Revision

How many birds (Ūsfoorah)s can you see in each picture? Write the Arabic number in the azraq أَزْرَقْ muthallath.

 Trace.

أ ب ت ث ج ح خ د ذ ر ز س ش ص ض ط ظ ع غ ف ق ك ل م ن هـ و ي

Lets write our homework !

Copy letter A'a أ inside the dresses.

Beginning

Middle

End

Lets write our homework !

 Copy the numbers.

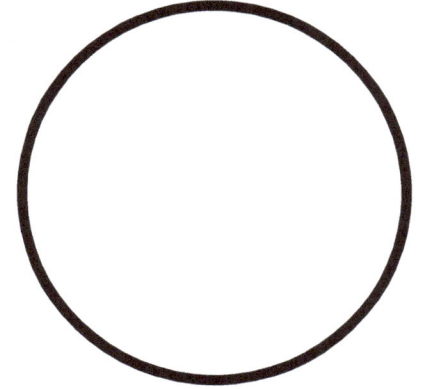 Color the muthallath ramaady and the rest of the shapes zahry.

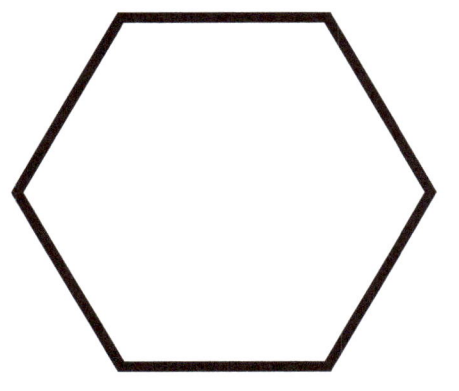
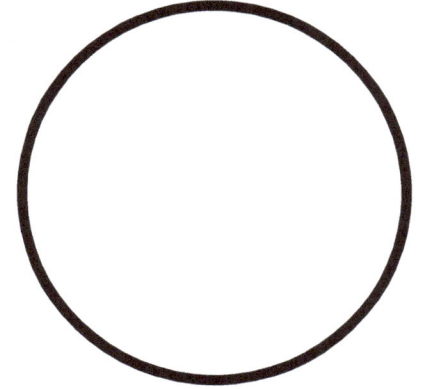

Lesson 5 : ب  Ba

Duck

We are sisters !

ب ت ث

  Battah

Remember

 Is a light and a friendly letter!

أ ب ت ث ج ح خ د ذ ر ز س ش ص ض ط ظ ع غ ف ق ك ل م ن هـ و ي

Trace letter Ba   ب   خَطِّطْ الْحَرْفْ

*Start writing from the right

Color letter ب at the beginning of each word Banafsajy.

57

© Arabic Joyride Press

ب Is a friendly letter

Look how it holds hands from both sides when joining in the middle of a word:

Now look how the letter ب gives only one hand from the front when it joins at the beginning of a word:

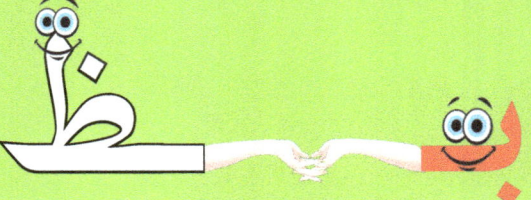

And finally, look how the letter ب gives only one hand from the back when joining at the end of a word:

أ ب ت ث ج ح خ د ذ ر ز س ش ص ض ط ظ ع غ ف ق ك ل م ن هـ و ي

The shapes of ba ب when joining

letter Ba can change dresses when joining other letters at the:

End   Middle   Beginning

Color letter Ba dresses :
at the beginning **burtuqaaly**, in the middle **aḥmar** and at the end **aṣfar**.

بَطَّةُ   جُبْنْ   عِنَبْ

 letter Ba ب with short vowels

With Fat-hah — Ba — ب

With Dammah — Bu — ب

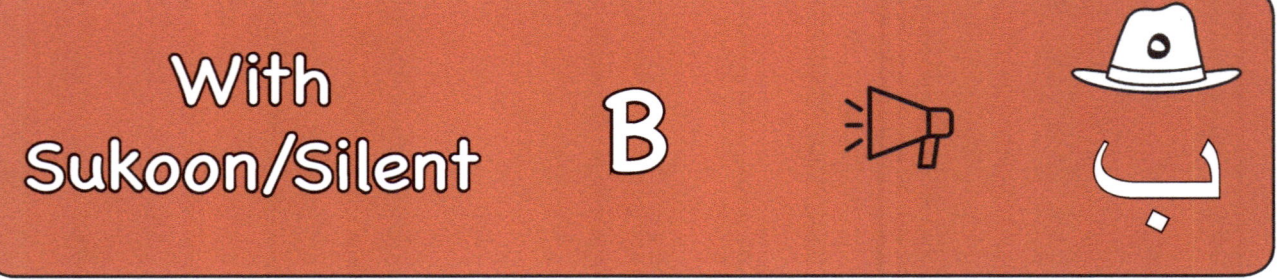

With Sukoon/Silent — B — ب

With Kasrah — Bi — ب

Match letter Ba بِ with its suitable hat or sock.

 Trace letter Ba with short vowels.

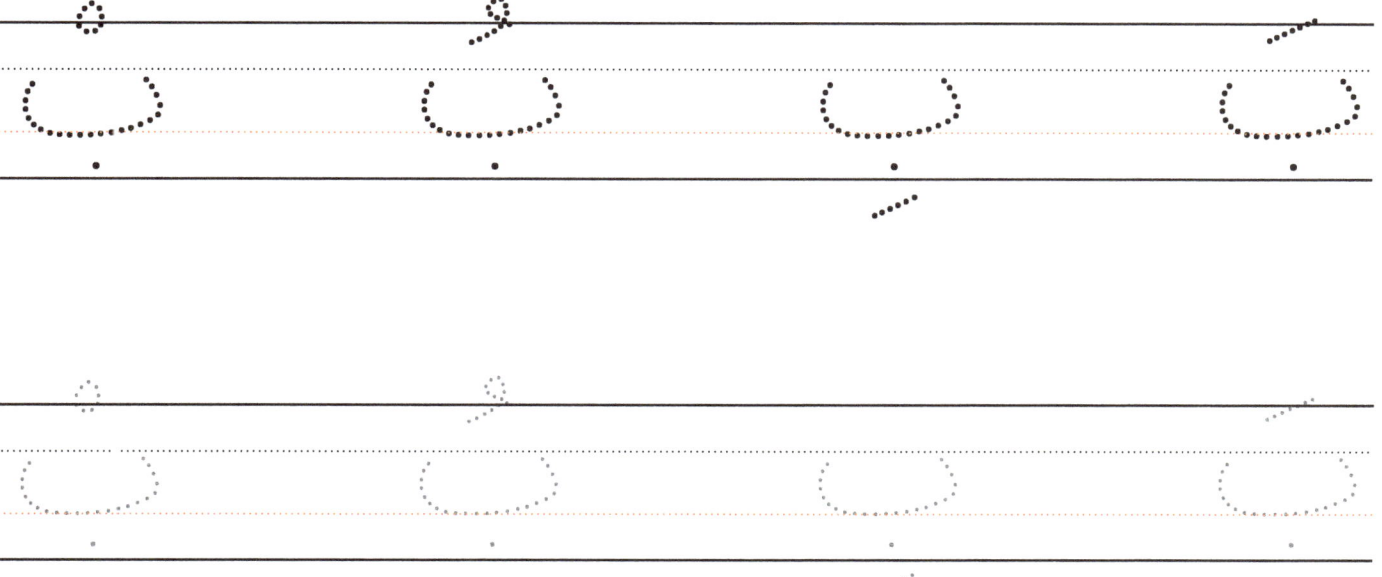

Match letter Ba with the correct word.

بِنْتٌ
Girl — Bint

بُسْتَان
Garden — Bustaan

كِتَاب
Book — Kitaab

بَيْتٌ
House — Bayt

بْ

بُ

بِ

بَ

Trace letter Ba ب at the beginning, middle and end.

The shapes in Arabic

Heart (Qalb - قَلْبٌ)

Color all (قَلْبٌ)s aḥmar and the rest of the shapes aswad.

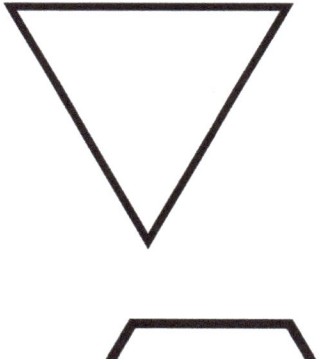

The Arabic numbers

Nine - Tisāah
تِسْعَة

Eight - Thamaaniyah
ثَمَانِيَة

 Trace.

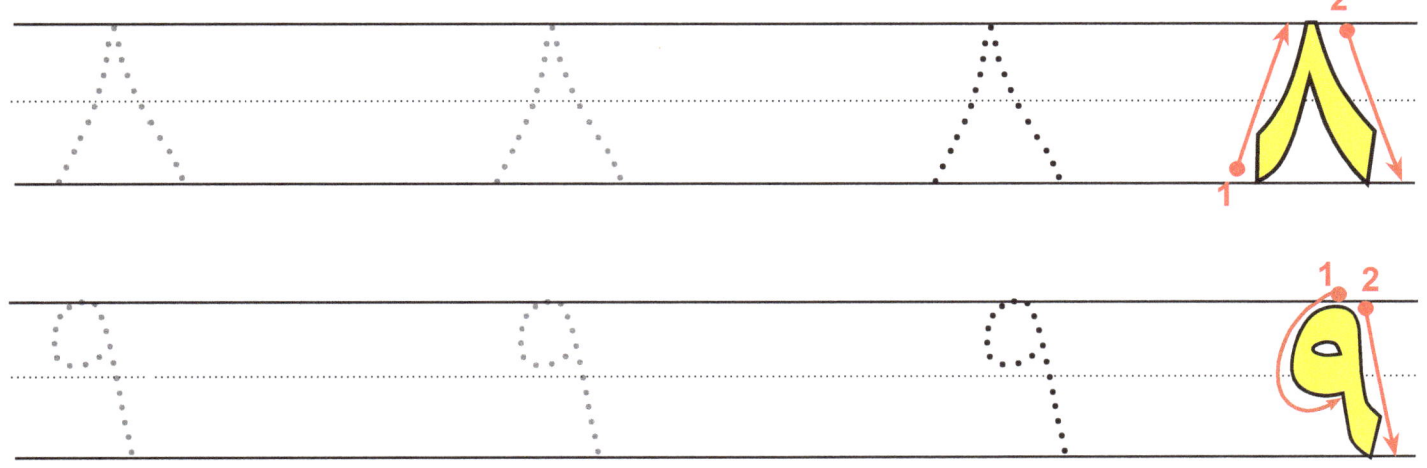

أ ب ت ث ج ح خ د ذ ر ز س ش ص ض ط ظ ع غ ف ق ك ل م ن هـ و ي

Revision

How many fish (Samakah)s can you see in each picture?

Trace.

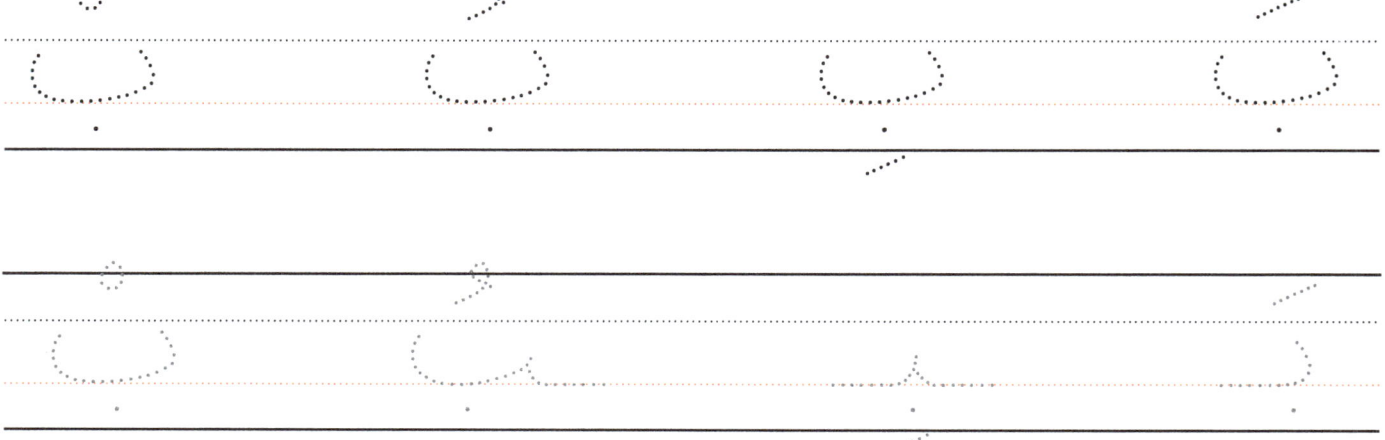

أ ب ت ث ج ح خ د ذ ر ز س ش ص ض ط ظ ع غ ف ق ك ل م ن هـ و ي

Lets write our homework !

Copy letter Ba ب inside the dresses.

Beginning

Middle

End

67
© Arabic Joyride Press

٢٠ ١٩ ١٨ ١٧ ١٦ ١٥ ١٤ ١٣ ١٢ ١١ ١٠ ٩ ٨ ٧ ٦ ٥ ٤ ٣ ٢ ١ ٠

Lets write our homework !

 Copy the numbers.

Color the qalb zahry
and the rest of the shapes azrzq.

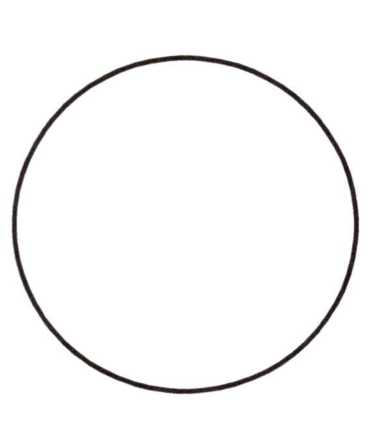 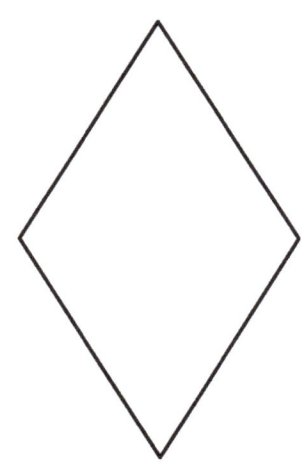 

68
© Arabic Joyride Press

Lesson 6 : ت 📢 Ta

Television

"We are sisters!"

 تِلْفَازْ       Tilfaaz

Remember

 Is a light and a friendly letter!

© Arabic Joyride Press

أ ب ت ث ج ح خ د ذ ر ز س ش ص ض ط ظ ع غ ف ق ك ل م ن هـ و ي

خَطَّطْ الحَرْفْ ت Trace letter Ta

*Start writing from the right

Color letter ت at the beginning of each word **bonny**.

ت Is a friendly letter

Look how it holds hands from both sides when joining in the middle of a word:

Now look how the letter ت gives only one hand from the front when it joins at the beginning of a word:

And finally, look how the letter ت gives only one hand from the back when joining at the end of a word:

أ ب ت ث ج ح خ د ذ ر ز س ش ص ض ط ظ ع غ ف ق ك ل م ن هـ و ي

The shapes of Ta ت when joining

letter Ta can change dresses when joining other letters at the:

Beginning

Middle

End

Color letter Ta dresses :
at the beginning **abyadh**, in the middle **zahry** and at the end **aswad**.

زَيْتْ

تُفَّاحْ

مَتْجَر

72

© Arabic Joyride Press

 letter Ta ت with short vowels

| With Fat-hah | Ta | 🔊 |  ت |

| With **D**ammah | Tu | 🔊 |  ت |

| With Sukoon/Silent | T | 🔊 |  ت |

| With Kasrah | Ti | 🔊 | 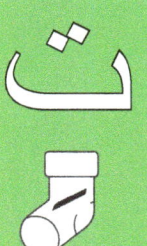 ت |

© Arabic Joyride Press

Match letter Ta ت with its suitable hat or sock.

Trace letter Ta with short vowels.

Match letter Ta with the correct word.

Student Tilmeeth
تِلْمِيذ

Dates Tamr
تَمْرْ

Apple Tuffaahah
تُفَّاحَة

Girl Bint
بِنْتْ

ت

ت

ت

ت

Trace letter Ta ت at the beginning, middle and end.

The shapes in Arabic

Hexagon (Sudaacy - سُدَاسِي)

Color all (سُدَاسِي)s banafsajy and the rest of the shapes asfar.

The Arabic numbers

Eleven - Iḥdaa āashar

إِحْدَى عَشَرْ

Ten - Āashrah

عَشْرَة

 Trace.

Revision

How many roses (Zahrah)s can you see in each picture?

 Trace.

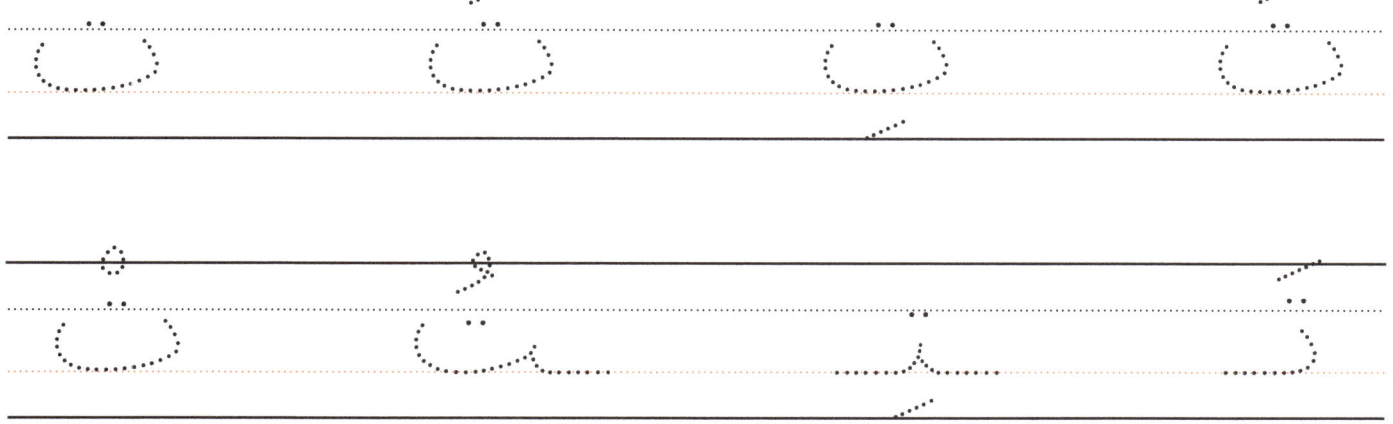

أ ب ت ث ج ح خ د ذ ر ز س ش ص ض ط ظ ع غ ف ق ك ل م ن هـ و ي

Lets write our homework !

Copy letter Ta ت inside the dresses.

Beginning

Middle

  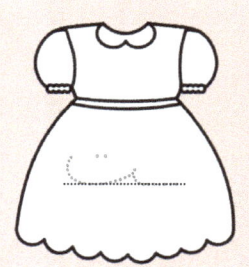 

End

Lets write our homework !

 Copy the numbers.

Color the sudaacy burtuqaaly and the rest of the shapes akhdar.

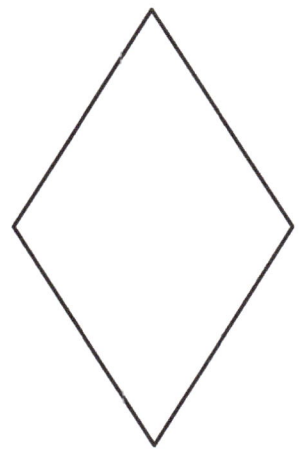

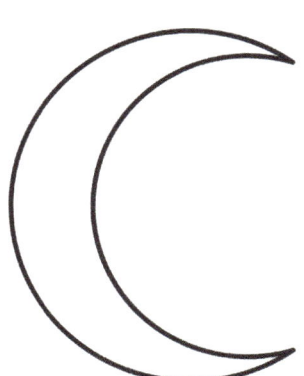

Lesson 7 : ث Tha

Snake

We are sisters !

ب   ت

 **Thuābaan**   ثُعْبَانٌ

Remember  Is a light and a friendly letter!

أ ب ت ث ج ح خ د ذ ر ز س ش ص ض ط ظ ع غ ف ق ك ل م ن هـ و ي

Trace letter Tha ث خَطِّطْ الحَرْفْ ث

*Start writing from the right

Color letter ث at the beginning of each word zahry.

  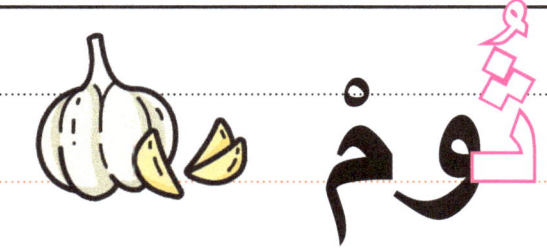

ث Is a friendly letter

Look how it holds hands from both sides when joining in the middle of a word:

Now look how the letter ث gives only one hand from the front when it joins at the beginning of a word:

And finally, look how the letter ث gives only one hand from the back when joining at the end of a word:

أ ب ت ث ج ح خ د ذ ر ز س ش ص ض ط ظ ع غ ف ق ك ل م ن هـ و ي

The shapes of Tha ث when joining

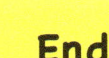 letter Tha can change dresses when joining other letters at the:

End	Middle	Beginning

Color letter Tha dresses :
at the beginning **azraq**, in the middle **asfar**
and at the end **burtuqaaly**.

بَحْثْ   مِثَالْ   ثَوْرْ

85
© Arabic Joyride Press

Match letter Tha with the correct word.

| With Fat-hah | Tha | 🔊 | ثَ |

| With Dammah | Thu | 🔊 | ثُ |

| With Sukoon/Silent | Th | 🔊 | ثْ |

| With Kasrah | Thi | 🔊 | ثِ |

Match letter Tha ث with its suitable hat or sock.

 Trace letter Tha with short vowels.

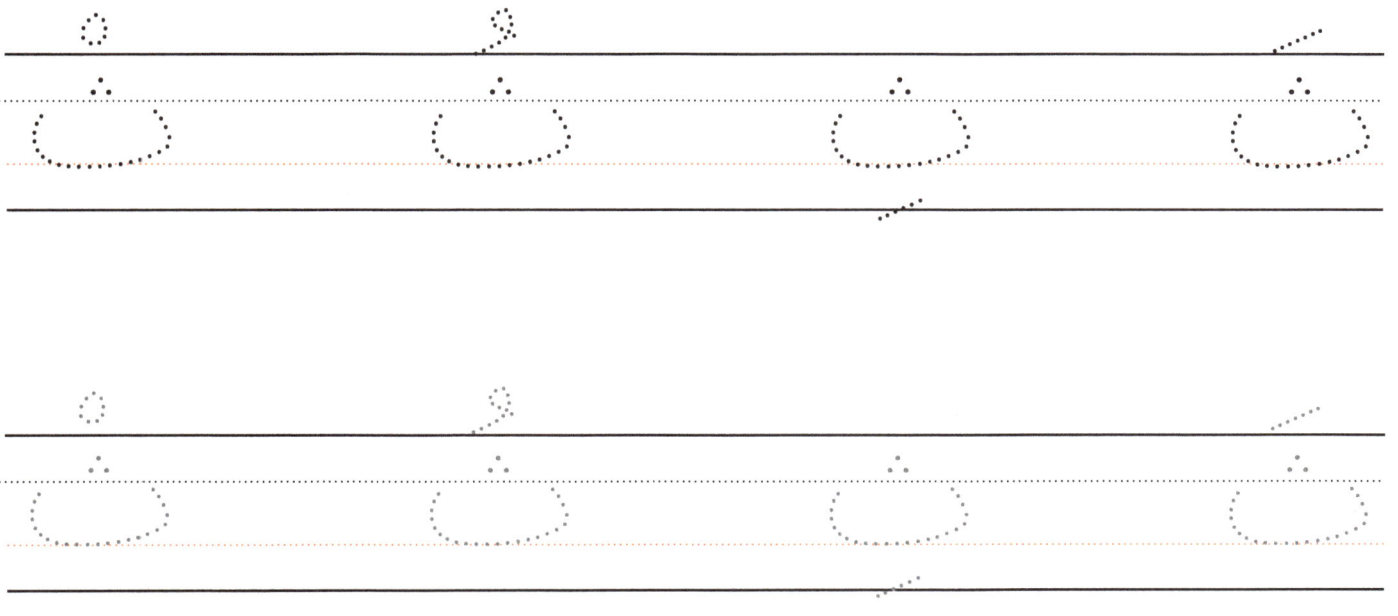

Match letter Tha with the correct word.

Lion — Layth

Hole — Thuqb

Clothes — Thiyaab

Ice — Thalj

© Arabic Joyride Press

Trace letter Tha at the beginning, middle and end.

The shapes in Arabic-Revision

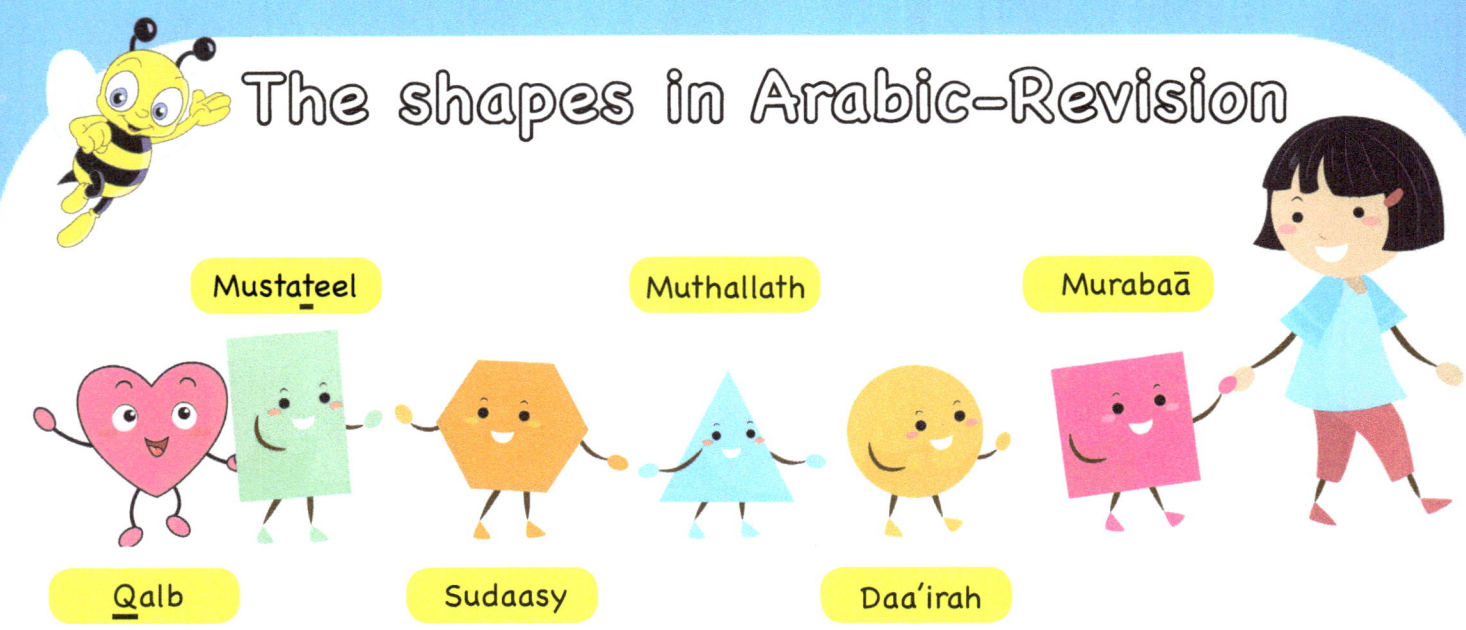

Color all (sudaacy)s ramaady, (daa'irah)s azraq, (muthallath)s bonny and (qalb)s ahmar.

The Arabic numbers

Thirteen - Thalaatha Āashar

ثَلَاثَ عَشَرْ

Twelve - Ithnaa Āashar

إِثْنَى عَشَرْ

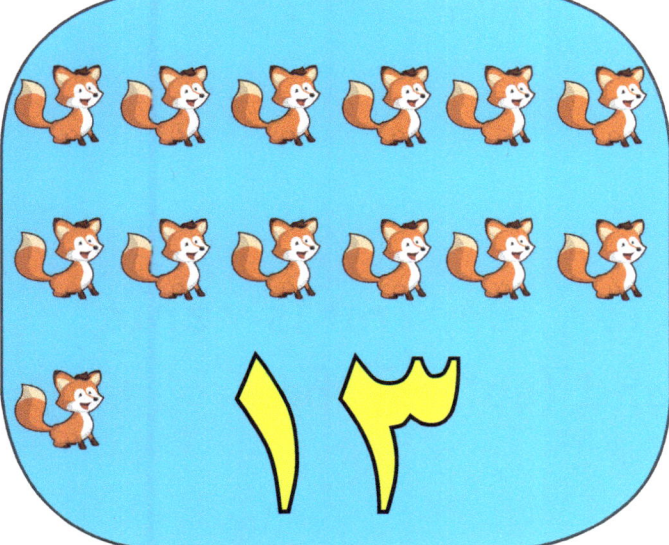

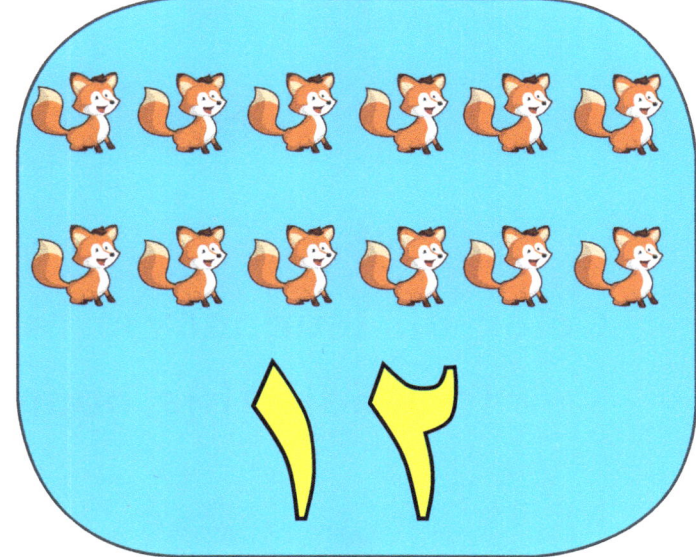

 Trace.

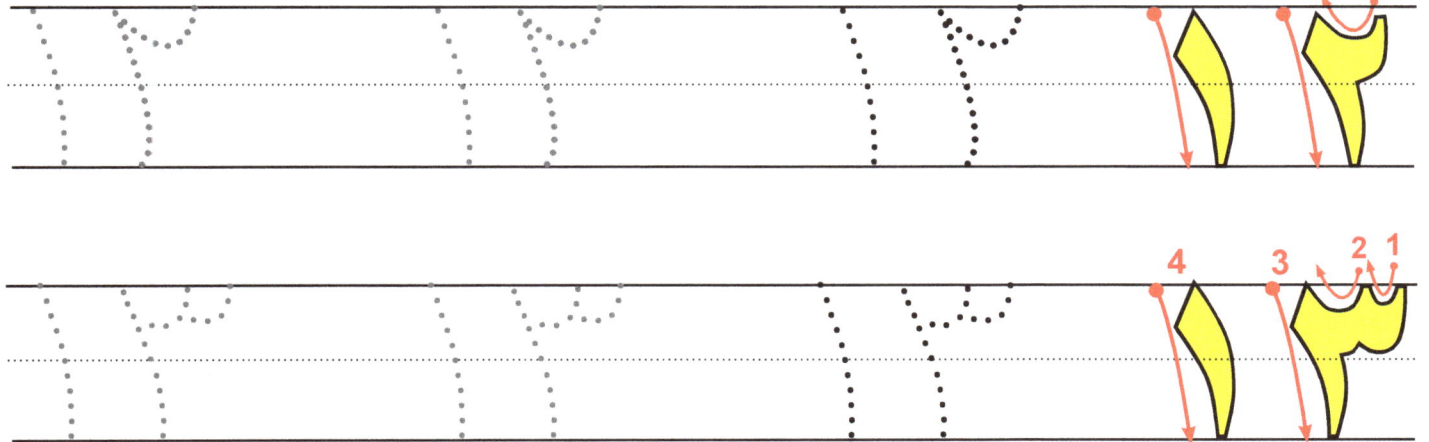

Revision

How many seagulls (nawras)s can you see in each picture?

 Trace

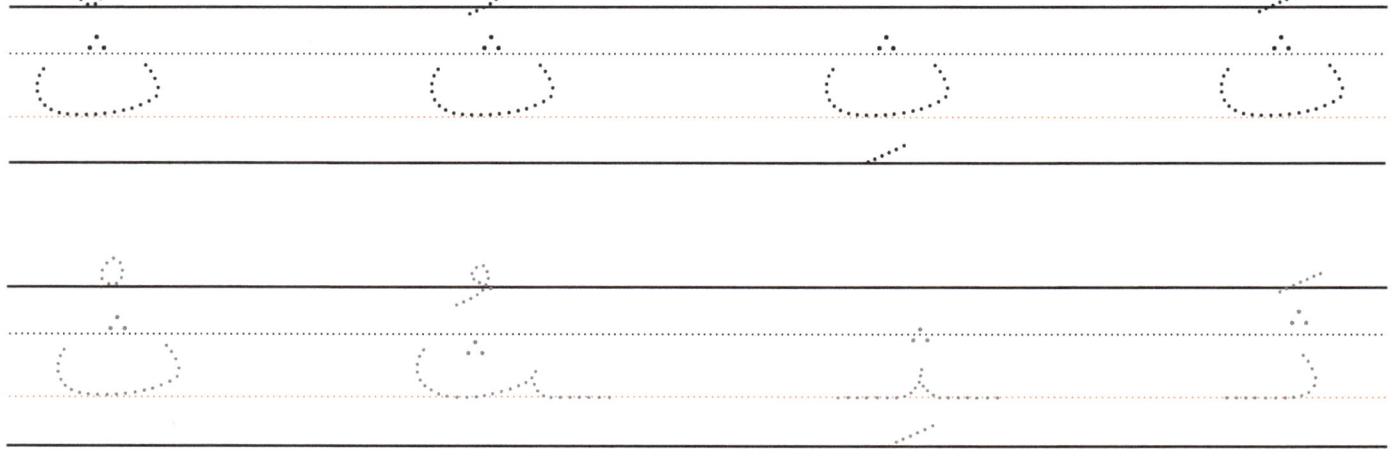

Lets write our homework !

Copy letter Tha ث inside the dresses.

Beginning

Middle

End

٢٠ ١٩ ١٨ ١٧ ١٦ ١٥ ١٤ ١٣ ١٢ ١١ ١٠ ٩ ٨ ٧ ٦ ٥ ٤ ٣ ٢ ١ ٠

Lets write our homework !

 Copy the numbers.

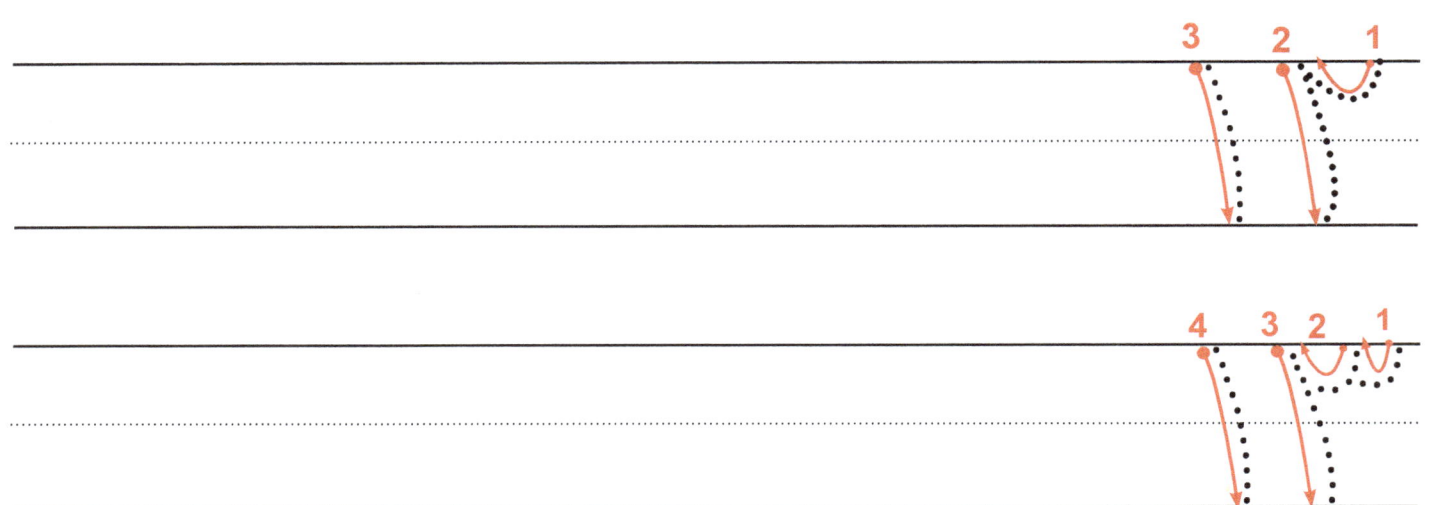

🖍️ Color the muthallath a<u>kh</u>dar and the rest of the shapes bonny.

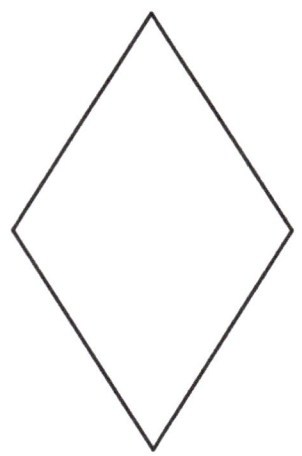
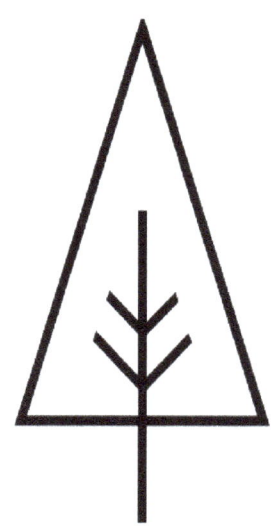
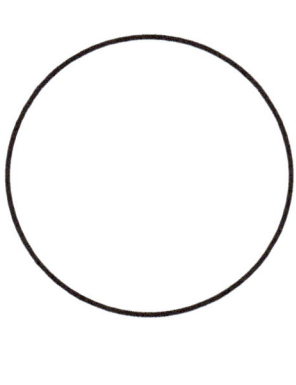

94

Lesson 8: Revision - trace.

Alphabet revision

Colour all the letters you learned in this book. Choose from the colours a<u>kh</u><u>d</u>ar, banafsajy, a̅hmar, burtu<u>q</u>aaly, bonny, a<u>s</u>far and azra<u>q</u>.

Numbers revision - trace.

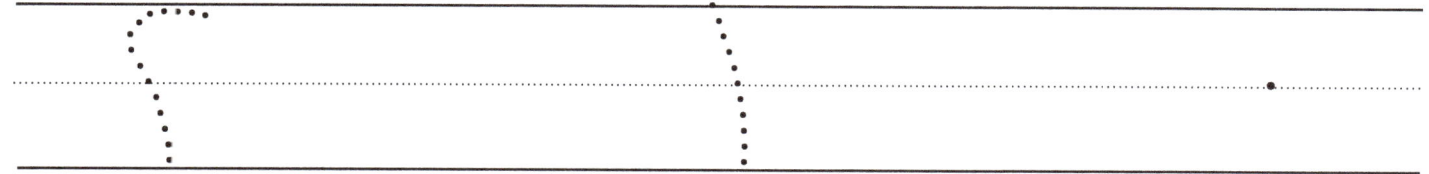
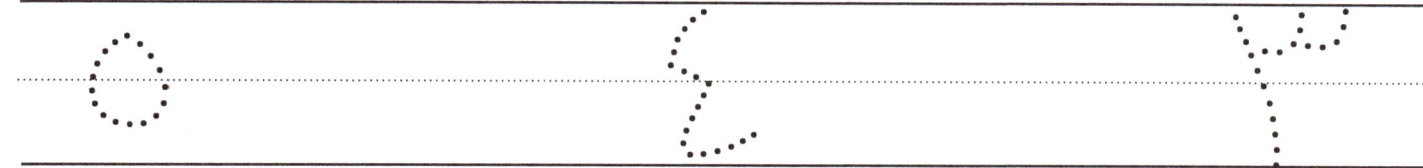
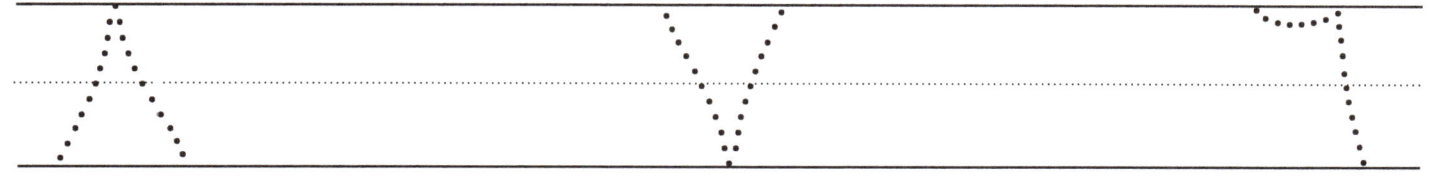
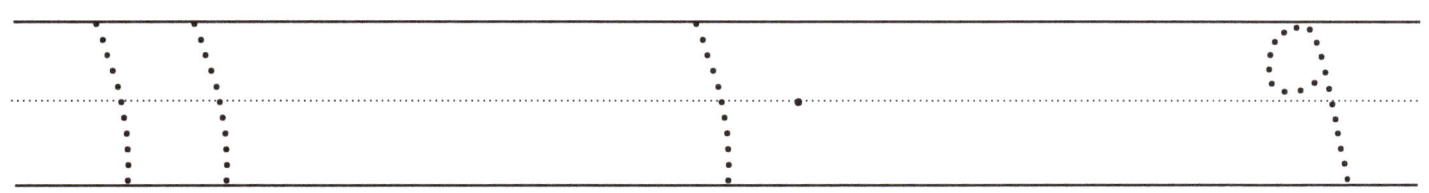

Numbers revision

Colour all the numbers you learned in this book. Choose from the colours a<u>kh</u>dar, banafsajy, a̅hmar, burtu<u>q</u>aaly, bonny, a<u>s</u>far and azra<u>q</u>.

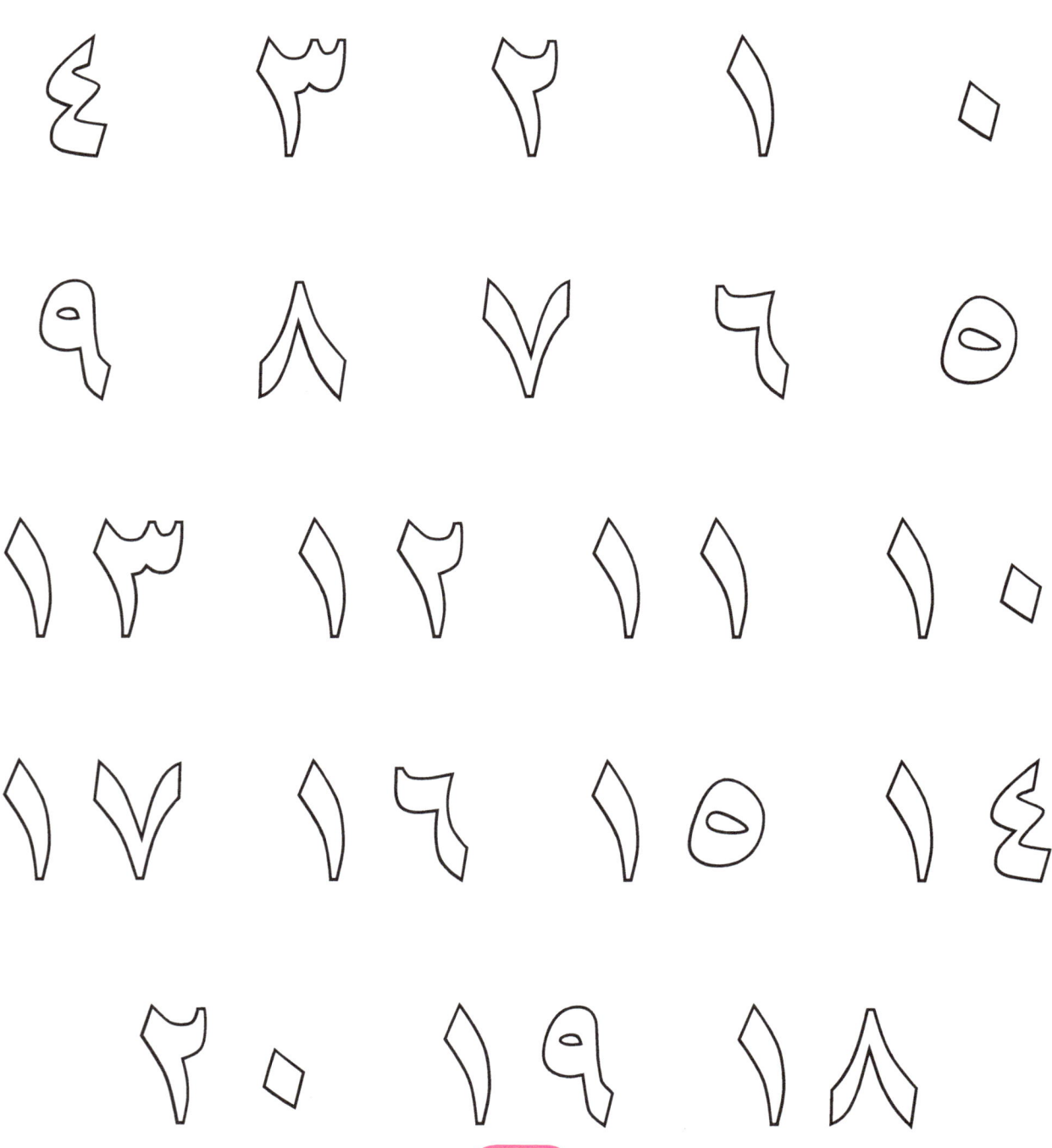

تم بحمد الله.

With Allah's grace, this workbook has been completed.

(وَقُلْ رَبِّ زِدْنِي عِلْمًا).

And say, My Lord, increase me in knowlede.